SNOWBIRD MATING SEASON

By Bernita Jackson Brown

Illustrated by
Paul Winer

I dedicate this book to Quartzsite, Arizona. To the hard working year round residents, as well as the Snowbirds, whose zest for life overflows and spreads like a virus every year during Snowbird Mating Season.

WHAT KIND OF PEOPLE MAKE UP THE HUGE THRONGS
WHO CONVERGE ON SOUTHERN ARIZONA IN THE
WINTER? WHAT KIND OF PEOPLE WILL POSSIBLY
TAKE PART IN ANYTHING CALLED "SNOWBIRD MATING
SEASON?"

Chapter One----When the autumn leaves have
been raked, the garden tools put away and the
golf course closed, instincts as old as time
tell the Snowbird to ready the nest for a
quick getaway. It's almost as if they can
hear the flapping wings, the quacks, honks,
and the errie cackles of thousands of
Snowbirds preparing to vee south for the
winter.

Chapter Two----It was 6:30 p.m. and we were
rolling down Interstate 10, five miles east
of our destination. The blaring CB radio was
tuned to Channel 19. All of a sudden a
confused trucker sounded off loud and clear,
"What in the hell's going on here? I
traveled through Quartzsite a couple of
months ago and this town was deader than a
squashed lizard. Look at all the campers,
there must be thousands of them."
        "Haven't you heard?" came the cheerful
reply, "It's Snowbird Mating Season."

Chapter Five----Like the Canadian Goose, the
Snowbird tends to be a heavy-bodied species.
When Snowbirds reach the age of 50 and
beyond, everything they eat starts developing
into what is known as the middle and lower
body, sometimes called middle-age spread.
The male, along with his long neck, sprouts a
large upper stomach while maintaining his
slim, skinny legs.
        The female bird adds to her beauty by
becoming more shapely. The bosoms, the hips,
stomach and legs rapidly blossom into what is
known as elegant maturity.

Best Wishes
B.J. Brown

SNOWBIRD MATING
SEASON

Edited by Jerra Davis and Jean Long

First Printing

Printed in the United States of America
by Pioneer Printing, Cheyenne, Wyoming

Snowbird Publishing
Rt. #1, Box 128B
Kimball, Nebraska 69145

ACKNOWLEDGEMENTS

First of all I want to give God all credit for any writing talent I may possess. Five years ago when facing a debilitating disease, and thinking I wouldn't be able to continue to play golf and enjoy life the way I wanted to, I prayed that God would show me what I could do with my spare time. Before that I had no idea that I had any talent for writing. The disease never developed, but I have learned that "I can do all things through Christ who strengthens me." Phil 4:13

Secondly I must thank our good friends Bill and Beryl Gustin. Without their retirement experiences, and having the courage to invite the rest of us to Arizona to take part in Snowbird Mating Season, there wouldn't be any book. Thanks also to the rest of our friends who have made up the characters in this book. The names have not been changed to protect the innocent because they are all guilty of enjoying life to the fullest.

I would like to thank Chuck Busby for the column he writes in the Quartzsite Gem. I borrowed his knowledge about the creatures of the desert and desert survival. Thanks also to T.J. Finley for allowing me to use his poems.

A special thanks to my husband Cork and all my family who have been neglected while I locked myself in the office this last year as I wrote the book. My elderly friends whom I visit through the church have also been neglected, my golf game has suffered, and who knows if I'll have any friends left, after they read this book.

Last, but not least, my good friends Jerra Davis and Jean Long who have spent long hours editing, and Paul Winer who has been such a joy to work with. God Bless you all.

CONTENTS

This book is being printed in large spacious
print for the benifit of my over 50 friends.

This Old House
(on Wheels)

Sitting up here
We can see all around
The crooked mountain roads
And each sleepy little town.

We don't have a time clock
To dictate our lives today
We just have a road map
To tell us where to play.

Some choose to live an R.V.
   life,
With a good spare tire
And a nice little wife.

Ridin' shotgun
Or in the driver's seat
Touring the country this way
Is awfully hard to beat.

Lots of lazy miles
Stretch out on ahead
We'll travel on today
Or we may just lie in bed.

This old country sure is pretty
So drink in deeply with your
   eyes
It's layed out in panorama
And becomes every traveller's
   prize.

At home our nice neighbors
Live up an' down our street
Out here we greet many new
   ones
As nice as you'll ever meet.

We have our kitchen and bath
We have our bedroom too
We may have a nice steak
Or just red beans and stew.

So from Lexington in the blue
   grass state
Or the woods of the state of
   Maine
From the cotton fields in the
   Southland
To the Mid-West's waving
   grain.

There are hotels and motels
From East to West
But our house on wheels
Is still the best.

T. J. Finley
© 1988

Chapter One

WHAT IS A SNOWBIRD?

Snowbirds are a special breed from the north country who can't stand the bite of the first frost, a sky full of grim clouds, or the weatherman predicting that first winter storm. Most Snowbirds are retired people who like to get away from near-artic winters and find a warm, cozy hide-a-way where the sun's rays can keep the arthritis to a minimum and exercise in the great outdoors can keep the body in shape and the cholesterol from clogging the arteries.

When the autumn leaves have been raked, the garden tools put away and the golf course closed, instincts as old as time tell them to ready the nest for a quick getaway. It's almost as if they can hear the flapping wings, the quacks, honks, and the errie cackles of thousands of Snowbirds preparing to vee south for the winter.

One of the favorite spots for winter nesting is Quartzsite, Arizona. Retired people from all over the United States and Canada descend on this small desert town in flocks that you will never believe, looking for a place in the sun.

Quartzsite lies quietly nestled between some of Arizona's most spectacular mountain ranges. It is located eighty miles north of Yuma at the crossroads of Highway 95 and Interstate 10. In summer the population is around 1800. When the Snowbirds converge it swells to 50,000.

In the Quartzsite area a Snowbird is defined as someone who has figured out how to take their nest with them and migrate south for the winter. Snowbirds can be likened to the Canadian geese who fly south with the same mate every year. The Snowbirds nest can be anything from the smallest pickup camper or tent to the largest $200,000 RV bus. Sometimes just a station wagon or a Volkswagen will make a nest for homeless people.

Sixty-four RV parks are scattered over a 36-mile area around Quartzsite. Parks are booked up a year in advance. The rest of the thousands of migrating Snowbirds need a place to roost. The U.S. Bureau of Land Management (BLM) has established eight Long Term Visitor Areas (LTVA) on public lands in the southern deserts of Arizona and California. Here Snowbirds in self-contained camping units can escape winter weather and heating costs. For an annual $25 permit fee, visitors can occupy a spot on Federal public lands for as long as seven months from September 15 to April 15 each year. There are some areas you can stay in free if you move every 14 days. Some people prefer solitude. You can find them parked way out in the desert by themselves. Snowbirds who stay in the LTVA'S are called boondockers.

The largest LTVA lies along U.S. 95 in Arizona's LaPaz County. It covers 11,000 acres immediately south of Quartzsite. There are four large camping areas. Campers must be self-contained. Showers and lavatories aren't furnished and camping is primitive, closer to nature. There are facilities for dumping sewer. Water can be bought in Quartzsite.

In the March 21, 1991, issue of the Quartzsite Gem, the local newspaper, was a thank you note from Leo Nencinia from Florence, Oregon. He said, "We wish to thank the city of Blythe, California, for all the free water, dumping station and garbage disposal that you have provided for us. To show our appreciation we do all of our shopping in Blythe." Blythe is 20 miles west of Quartzsite. Snowbirds do have a choice as to where they can do their shopping, dumping and refilling.

If you have ever seen the Canadian geese and the Sandhill cranes, who come by the thousands to use the North Platte river and surrounding cornfields between Grand Island and Kearney, Nebraska, for a feeding ground and roosting place on their way north in the springtime, you will have a perception of what Quartzsite, Arizona, looks like during Snowbird Mating Season. Both are a spectacular sight to behold, two of Mother Nature's wonders.

It's not just the weather that attracts Snowbirds to this small desert town. Quartzsite is the home of the famous "Pow

Wow", the largest Rock and Gem Show in this
country. It is sponsored by the Quartzsite
Improvement Association (QIA), a volunteer
organization of mostly Snowbirds. Each year
the Pow Wow runs the first week in February,
starting on the first Wednesday. Inside the
8,500 square foot building are some of the
best dealers selling gems, jewelry, and rock
related items. You will also see more than
60 display cases showing carved gems from
around the world. Five hundred dealers set
up shop outside the QIA building which houses
the show. There are daily field trips and
the largest operating display of lapidary
equipment in the country. Dealers come from
many states as well as Canada, Great Britain,
Brazil and Australia. It has been estimated
that over 1,000,000 people visit Quartzsite
the week of the big Pow Wow.

The Pow Wow isn't the only attraction.
Starting mid-January the world's largest swap
meets take place in Quartzsite. Block after
block, acre after acre of trucks, campers and
buses set up as far as the eye can see.
Dealers and artists arrange their booths
under the awning of their motorhomes and sell
everything imaginable, such as antiques and
good classy junque. The general theme is
rocks and gems, jewelry, arts and crafts,
much better than the average swap meet.

When the typical Snowbird couple arrives
here, their first purchase is a bumper
sticker that reads, "I'm spending my
children's inheritance." John and LaVern
Cathey have been Snowbirds for 15 years.
They pass out a calling card with the
following verse: "The clock of time is wound
but once, and no man has the power to tell
just when the hands will stop on what day or
what hour. Now is the only time you have, so
live it with a will, don't wait until
tomorrow, the hands may then be still." John
says, "I don't even buy green bananas

anymore. I'm afraid they won't get ripe before I die." This seems to be the motto of the Snowbirds as they try to pack as many activities as they can into each day. They wander up and down the aisles of the shows until they're exhausted. Then they go to the nest, relax and store enough energy for the next day.

There are at least five huge shows and several smaller ones going on before and after the Pow Wow. One of the shows, The Main Event, encompasses 30 acres. There are over 1,000 tailgaters selling their wares. "Top vendors from all over the continent bring their best to the Quartzsite celebration," says Howard Armstrong, Main Event promoter.

In the next few chapters I will take you on a trip to the middle of Quartzsite, Arizona, and beyond. We'll spend several weeks as a boondocker, then relax in a classy RV Resort. We'll take a look at what kind of people make up the huge throngs who converge on southern Arizona in the winter time. What kind of people will possibly take part in anything called "Snowbird Mating Season"?

Chapter Two

ARIZONA HERE WE COME

Our best friends, nearing the ripe old age of 54, decided they couldn't take the rat race anymore. They had been employed in the oilfields for thirty-five years and owned their own trucking business. They listed the business and their house for sale, purchased a motorhome, and took off for Arizona.

Everybody thought they were crazy, including us. Beryl kept busy with bowling, crocheting, playing bridge and golf. Bill was devoted to his business and spent long hours trucking around the country. He also had a deep love for fishing and hunting, and entertained many customers at the lake or the duck blind. Being on call night and day for many years had taken its toll. He was tired. But, how can they possibly give it all up to go south and sit in the sun?

"They must be losing their marbles, they're too young to retire, they'll go stark raving mad sitting around looking at each other," my husband, Cork, said.

"What about us? How can they possibly go off and leave all their friends? There goes my bridge partner and my golf partner, and who are we going to get to bowl in her place?" I asked.

"Our bridge foursome will never be the same without Beryl," Beverly said. "She's the only one I know that can make yummy banana bread. One day she forgot to mash the banana into the batter so she put a whole one in the middle and baked it that way. It sure was good."

"I know Bill will never be able to give up his fishing trips to Canada," Dick said. "You just wait and see, they'll be back. Ol' Billy Boy couldn't stand to think of us up there catching those big lake trout without him. Besides, who'll do our cooking?"

Despite all our crying, moaning and prophesying, they headed south anyhow. Bill said, "I have worked through my last snowstorm, scooped my last shovel of snow and worn my last pair of long-johns. I'm going to tie my snow shovel on the back of this motorhome and travel south until someone asks me what it is. That's where I'm going to retire." Off they went, leaving the rest of us to batten down the hatches, and dig in for another long, snowing, blowing Nebraska winter.

Bill and Beryl discovered Yuma, Arizona, well known as a Snowbird haven. They settled down, bought a house complete with swimming

pool, a condo and an apartment house. They
sat back and relaxed, knowing the income from
their rental places and interest from their
investments would support them very well. It
wasn't long until we started receiving
letters about their escapades in the desert.
They were searching all over the desert for
rocks, coin hunting and working their tails
off dry-washing for gold.

Beryl was thrilled about their new life,
and tried to portray it to us by way of
letter. "This is a perfect place for your
winter vacation," Beryl wrote. "Finding a
special rock and cutting it open is just like
opening a package at Christmastime. You
never know what your going to find," she
added.

I answered her saying we were having
trouble getting interested in a bunch of
rocks. In my wildest imagination I couldn't
picture us wandering around in the desert all
day looking for pretty rocks. The thought of
rattle snakes, cactus and blowing sand turned
me off. "If they will guarantee we can find
a gold mine, we might get excited," Cork
said.

One day as Beryl and Bill were driving
north of Yuma, they stumbled into a town
called Quartzsite. It was at the crossroads
of Highway 95 and Interstate 10, supposedly
just a wide spot in the road. They wrote
trying to describe the sight as they entered
the little town.

"We were surprised to see so many campers
and motorhomes parked all over the desert,"
Beryl said. They passed another motorhome
from Nebraska. He invited them, by way of
the CB to a gathering of Nebraska people.
They didn't attend the Nebraska picnic, but
found a place to park and stayed three days.

"You just won't believe it. It's
impossible to describe. It's a big Rock and
Gem Show, and people come from all over the

world for this event," Beryl said. "There
are motorhomes parked as far as the eye can
see."

I still can't see myself playing around
with rocks. I wear hardly any jewelry, what
will I do with rocks and gems if I have them?
Our chances of finding gold are less than our
chance of winning the lottery or the Reader's
Digest Sweepstakes. At least with the
lottery you don't have to participate with a
pick and shovel. Of course there is more
exercise in shoveling.

After listening for three years to their
stories about the big deal going on in this
little town, we agreed to meet them in
Quartzsite during the show. We had our trip
all planned. We were going to visit a couple
of weeks with friends in Palm Springs,
California. We wanted to spend our time
playing golf, laying in the sun where
swimming pools were plentiful, the grass was
green, the lakes were blue and the flowers
bloomed all winter.

On our way home we met Beryl and Bill six miles south of Quartzsite at N. 53rd St. We slept in the back of the van. It was frosty cold and I thought I was going to freeze my buns without any heat. "I thought it was supposed to be warm in this country," I complained.

We wandered around in one Rock Show all day and never did see it all. We were tired by three o'clock and went back to camp. We didn't have a bonfire because we didn't know where to look for wood. We were surprised to find the floor of the desert so level. In places it was like a paved street. To keep warm after dark, and after a few beers, we turned on the stereo and danced to country western music. The next afternoon, after a few more beers we took out our golf clubs and hit old golf balls amongst the rocks, the greasewood bushes, the jumping cactus and the saguaro. It was the first time we had played a course that was all sand trap.

"I'm sorry, but I'm having trouble enjoying this after spending two weeks with the plush courses in Palm Springs," Cork said. We only stayed two days. Hardly enough time to see everything they wanted to show us.

After several years of visiting the Oasis in the Desert called Palm Springs, and living the life of the rich for two to three week vacations, we decided we wanted to try a motorhome and see more of how the middle-class people of this world were spending their retirement and vacations. We knew we would probably never be able to retire and live the lifestyle of the wealthy. We purchased a used motorhome and set our bearings for Quartzsite, Arizona.

It was 6:30 p.m. and we were rolling down Interstate 10, five miles east of our destination. The blaring CB radio was tuned to Channel 19. All of a sudden a confused trucker sounded off loud and clear, "What in the hell's going on here? I traveled through Quartzsite a couple of months ago and this town was deader than a squashed lizard. Look at all the campers, there must be thousands of them."

"Haven't you heard?" came the cheerful reply. "It's Snowbird Mating Season."

It was a dazzling sight coming into town in the evening. The motorhomes were all gathered together in groups. Wagons were circled like the Conestogas of yesteryear, with a large bonfire in the middle. The hot orange flames from the camps reached up to tickle the sky blue heavens and blend with the red-tinged setting sun. This small part of the world was aglow with the sounds and sights of thousands of senior citizens having the time of their lives.

Chapter Three

WILD GOOSE CHASE

Arriving in Quartzsite after dark wasn't the smartest thing we accomplished that day. Beryl wrote and told us exactly where they would be. She said, "Take the East exit off of I-10 and follow Business 10 to the four-way stop. Turn left on Highway 95, proceed over the bridge and take the first street to the East. We'll be on the left side. I'll tie a yellow ribbon on the antenna so you'll be sure to spot us from a distance."

No problem. With simple directions like that how could we get lost? We found our way to the four-way stop, through the heavy traffic, and turned left to proceed over the bridge. We inched our way to the top of the overpass only to hear the screaming siren of an ambulance. There wasn't any place to pull over or stop. We finally reached the south side of the bridge and eased off to the right to let the ambulance go by.

"Now," I said, "they should be right here to the left." We looked around only to find ourselves in the middle of a show area called Tyson's Sell-A-Rama. "We must have made a wrong turn some place," I told Cork.

"Of course we did, we were supposed to turn left on this side of the bridge, we'll turn around here and get back across the highway," he said.

We managed the turn around, then had to wait for the speeding fire trucks to whiz by. Driving in this traffic is like roller skating in a buffalo herd. We proceeded across the road and Cork turned to the right side to ask for information at the check-in point for campers. Our group was planning to dry camp close to town for $3 a night so we could walk to the shows. The man in charge didn't have anyone listed from Kimball, Nebraska, or Yuma, Arizona. Other friends from Kimball, Wyoming, Oregon and California were also planning to meet us here. We were going to have our own gathering of Snowbirds.

"There are two different camps here, we're supposed to be on the left side," I said.

"No, we're not, Beryl said right. Get out and look around and see if you can spot an antenna with a yellow ribbon. We know their motorhomes. This should be a simple task," he barked.

We walked around, then drove around for another hour, snapping and growling at each other like a couple of dogs. Every motorhome was bedecked with yellow ribbons! At least 2,000 of them in this small area were showing their support of our troops in the Gulf. The American flag was gallantly flying from every camper, large or small, combined with the yellow ribbons. We were touched by the patriotism the Snowbirds were showing for our country and our troops.

With tears in my eyes I calmly told Cork, "Next to the war, our little problem isn't worth fussing and fighting about. So, what if we have to park out in the desert by ourselves tonight. Maybe we should kiss and

make up. If this is Snowbird Mating Season,
we're not off to a very good start."

"I'm all for making up, but if you don't
mind, let's find a place to roost for the
night first," he answered.

That's my mate, never romantic when I
want him to be. Cork tried the noisy CB one
more time without any results. We drove back
to Highway 95, turned south and started
looking for one of the Long Term Visitor
Areas to find a piece of real estate that
wasn't already occupied for the evening. One
thing for sure, nobody will ever have to be
alone in this bustling jungle of people.

As we aimlessly wandered around looking
for a place to park, we noticed creative
signs of all kinds marking the way for lost
birds to find their flocks. "Wouldn't it be
nice if our flock left a sign for us?" I
asked. "At least they could hang a paper
plate on a greasewood bush."

As we maneuvered our way in and around
the camping areas Cork called my attention to
the moon. "Look," he said, "It really is
Snowbird Mating Season." The bright orange
moon was peering over the mountain, full and

happy as a smiling pumpkin. We pulled into the first empty spot, resigned to the fact that our flock would be waiting for us tomorrow.

We lay in bed that night looking at the moon and listening to the far off cry of a howling coyote and a strumming guitar, knowing that we weren't alone. We were right at home among 50,000 other Snowbirds, asleep in our own nest here in God's country.

The next morning we were awakened as the sunlight poured in the windows, rushing through the cracks in the shades. We devoured a quick, healthy, home-cooked breakfast of cold cereal, one of my favorite meals to cook, then continued our search for the lost flock.

The motorhome hummed like a contented kitten as we pulled onto Highway 95, heading back to the area we had been so ably instructed to find. This time we tried the left side of the road. There to our amazement was a paper plate tied to a greasewood bush, pointing the way to our assembling group. I wanted to say, "I told you so," but bit my tongue. After all, it's Snowbird Mating Season. A good reason to be on my most pleasant behavior.

We were the fifth motorhome to arrive and took our place in the circle that was already forming. Jeri and Maxine, and Will and Dee from California, Bill and Beryl from Yuma, and John and LaVern from our hometown of Kimball were already there, patiently waiting for us. We bounded out of the motorhome to get hugs all around. Seeing friends just once a year makes for a cheerful reunion.

There was still work to do before the nest was ready for roosting. Usually we have to level the motorhome, but the level floor of the desert eliminated that chore. Since we would be boondocking without any hookups, all we had to do was light the hot water heater, get out the welcome mat, the lawn chairs and the picnic table.

Bill hollered, "All you hairy-legged boys get in the pickup, we're going farther out in the desert to see if we can find some dead ironwood for the campfire." Jeri remained sitting, mumbling something about not having hair on his legs.

It's the female snowbird's job to search for big enough rocks to make a fire ring. Then she is expected to dig a hole in the middle of the ring to make room for the build-up of ashes. Blowing ashes can cause a fire hazard.

In the Quartzsite Gem that very morning was a picture of three burning motorhomes. If you have ever seen the charred ruins and the heartache of three families left without a home, and all their belongings laying in a pile of rubble, you will understand the importance of a proper campfire.

Being greenhorns about camping in a motorhome, we had a lot to learn. We waited around for the rest of the group to tell us what was next. My experiences with camping up until this time were not pleasant. But with this motorhome everything was going to be just like home. My idea of roughing it is turning the thermostat down to 70 degrees and having only one small bathroom. Bathrooms in motorhomes aren't made for the heavy-bodied Snowbird. But, I can cope if that's what is required for being a "happy camper".

Tyson's Sell-A-Rama was starting and we wanted to hurry over there before someone else beat us to the bargains. We had already missed out on the first few days at the Main Event. "We'll make up for lost time," Beryl assured us as she came out of her motorhome with a purse on a belt around her waist.

"What's that for?" I asked.

"You carry this instead of a heavy purse. Your shoulders will break if you carry that enormous bag. You have to know how to travel light and fast, we have a lot of ground to cover. Snowbirds have to be in good shape or they don't survive the flight, you know. One of these fanny packs can be your first purchase."

Well, I don't know if I can handle this. "I thought the flight down here was the hardest part. Now you tell me my body has to be in good shape. This is one Snowbird that's in trouble," I mumbled.

Chapter Four

A DAY AT TYSON'S SELL-A-RAMA

    LaVern came out of her motorhome with a backpack and dragging a wire pull cart like old ladies take to the grocery store when they are walking.

    "Now, what is all that for?" I asked

    "We always pull a cart to haul our purchases around. We'll be walking to Tyson's today, so we'll need all the help we can get. You can't count on the guys for anything. They disappear about the time you need something carried," LaVern said.

"Surely my husband won't do that, it's Snowbird Mating Season! They're supposed to be nice to us or we'll look around and find us a new gander," I said.

"Is a gander anything like a sugar daddy?" LaVern wanted to know.

"Something like that," I answered.

Now that I was all educated on what was needed to survive the day, we took off walking, in and around the green-barked Palo Verde trees and the lacey-leafed mesquite bushes, down into a wash. In Nebraska we call them dry creek beds. In Arizona they are known as washes because when it rains, it pours, and the desert floor is as hard as cement. Water won't soak into the ground. It all runs into a low area called a wash.

Beryl was explaining, "If you ever get caught out in a rainstorm, stay away from the washes or you'll drown." I was trying to file all this information away for future use. If we were going to spend time in the desert we needed to know all the rules of survival.

"Watch out for bear traps," John said.

"I didn't know they had bears here, they don't really do they? Why would they put traps out here where people walk?" I asked.

"He's just trying to be funny. He's talking about dog poop piles," LaVern said.

Leave it to me to step in the first smart crack of the day. "Just wait, your turn's coming," I hollered back at John.

We walked through a storm drain, under the highway, and into the area called Tyson's Sell-A-Rama. I decided to people watch that first day. I knew enough about shopping in general to know that it was O.K. to just look at the merchandise and return later, on the way home, to pick up anything you couldn't live without. Watching people was one of my

favorite pastimes.   I   was   having   trouble
believing there could possibly be this many
crazy people in   one   place.   But, there they
were right before my eyes.

I never will understand why people   bring
their dogs to a congested area like this, but
they   were   everywhere.   Big   wolf   hounds
lunging at little terriers like they wanted
to eat them for lunch.   I don't have anything
against dogs, but   I hate to step on them, or
in   their   piles.   One   time   when   we   were
traveling with another couple in a motorhome,
I got up in the middle of the night and
stepped in a real gooey mess that oozed up
between my toes!   "OH! SHIIIT!" I screamed.
My   mate bolted to an upright position as
if he'd been shot, and shouted, "What is it?"
"I stepped in it," I answered.
The   dog knew he was in trouble   and   was

wanting to go outside. I hopped on one foot
to the door and let him out.   It wouldn't
have been so bad but the owner of the dog was
laying in the other room giggling like a
laughing hyena all the while I hobbled into
the bathroom, stuck my size nine foot in the
size five sink and gave it a bath.

One guy had the right idea. His dog had
on a sun visor and was being pushed in a baby
stroller. I presume he had a diaper on his
baby, too.

People who live in the desert year round
are sometimes called desert rats, as well as
boondockers. On this particular day I saw a
dirty sun-scorched, older man with a young
scraggly-haired girl, carrying a baby. And a
younger couple dressed in buckskins with
three dirty-faced kids clinging to mom's
skirt, or running along behind. I wondered
why they weren't in school or if school is
even a part of their life. Then I saw a
young man with full beard, skin leathered
from the sun, a guitar over his shoulder and
all his belongings, in a Volkswagen,
including a big dog. I guess he is never
alone as long as he has his best friend and
his music.

Another young man was traveling alone
with his whole world on a bicycle. "I know
why he doesn't have a woman along, she'd
never be able to get her whole world on a
bike," my husband said.

And then there was a long-haired, dirty,
young man who was talking on the phone I was
waiting to use. He was calling the Salvation
Army, somewhere, asking for help. I thought
of him as a boy because he was about the same
age as my sons at home. Even though they are
in their thirtys they are still my boys.
Somewhere there is a mother who is wondering
where this boy is. Seeing some of the people
who live in this area who are homeless and
needy made me realize how important our

family and flock of friends are to us. I
grew tired of waiting to use the phone and
wandered off to look at another booth.
   I started thinking about the boy again
and went back to the phone booth only to find
him gone. It made me think about the many
gifts God has bestowed on us, and how there
are times that it wouldn't hurt me to share
some of what I have with others. Hopefully I
will get another chance. Do homeless people
like their life the way it is? I don't know.

One man with a full bushy beard and skin as
taut as a crudely stitched moccasin, from a
lifetime of living under the sun, maneuvered
his way among the senior citizens making his
way from one vendor to the next attempting to
barter his findings for a blanket to keep him
warm.

The graveled aisles were packed as people ran from one booth to the other. The sun was starting to beat down and the sweaters came off and into the pull carts. It felt warm and exhilarating to run around in a short sleeve shirt in February. Knowing the danger of cancer from the sun, we were all wearing hats or visors to keep the sun off the nose and face, but we needed to get some Vitamin D from the sun if we were going to survive life in the fast lane. Most retired people are looking for the slow lane, but there isn't time during Snowbird Mating Season in Quartzsite, unless you're waiting in line or traveling on Business 10.

My husband and 100 other men stopped off in a booth that was selling tools and war surplus items. They were worse than women shoppers, pushing and shoving.

The female Snowbirds' first stop was at a craft booth that was selling red, blue and yellow ribbons, with a small American flag attached. We each pinned one on to show support for our fighting troops. Maxine and Jeri had a son serving in the Gulf, on the ship the U.S. Shasta.

I soon found a fanny pack and a back pack and was outfitted for the duration of our stay. Tee shirts and sweatshirts were a big selling item, along with crafts of all kinds. You could buy the material to make your own, or buy the finished project.

Rocks and jewelry of all kinds were in every other booth. My favorite rocks were the amethyst and the quartz. The quartz crystal, in long fingers, glittered like huge diamonds in an expensive jewelry store. The amethyst looked like clusters of grapes dangling over a stone wall. They came in huge greyish-green rocks called geodes and, when opened, revealed the clusters. I was fascinated by the smoked crystal. When I asked what it was and where it came from, I was told that it is Arkansas crystal. Some of it isn't quite as sparkly and shiny as the rest, so they send it off to be cobalted and can sell it for more money. I might add here that I know nothing about rocks and wasn't sure yet whether I wanted to learn, but the more you hang around at rock shows the more fascinating rocks become.

Since our motorhome was new, at least to us, I headed for a booth selling everything you will ever need or want for a motorhome or trailer. We bought a dish drainer, rubber, spongy, non-slip mats, a refrigerator fan, dish pans, florescent lights, chemical for the toilet, and the list goes on. I had Beryl and LaVern's cart full before we left the first row! For a minute I forgot that I was only going to people watch.

Cork went crazy and bought an awning from Carefree Awnings of Colorado. They use their own installers and would have our awning on our motorhome at four o'clock, if they could only find us in this growing flock of Snowbirds. The awning salesmen were also selling windshield covers and tire covers to keep the sun out and off of your motorhome. "We don't need a windshield cover, I came here to soak up the sun, not try to keep it away," I said.

Then Cork wandered over to look at TV satellite dishes for RV's. I squawked like a wounded duck. "We're not buying a TV dish. If we want to sit and watch TV, we can stay at home. Your antenna works just fine." He kept looking anyway.

It is quite evident as you walk up and down the aisles, that the mating call of the Snowbird is somewhat different than the ordinary bird. Definitely different from the Canadian goose. I wasn't the only lady Snowbird trying to call her mate. The air was filled with sweet nothings being shouted back and forth across the aisles. "Honey,

Honey,   bring   me   some   money,"   one   lady
hollered. About 15 men ran the other way...
as fast as retired men can run.
     Or   listening   to   the   patient   and
consistent moan of a gander, "I'm not going
down that row one more time. I've had it!"
     His wife's understanding   answer,   "Good,
you just stay right there, or go on to camp.
I can find my own way home. I told you to
get in shape for this before we left home,
now you can't keep up. If you're going dear,
please leave me some money."
     Then there's the sweet, affectionate call
of the female Snowbird, "Honey, would you buy
this for me?"
     "Of course, dear, you give me the money
and I'll buy it," came the reply.
     Snowbirds have nicknames for their mates
and if you listen closely while walking
around the shows you can pick up the mating
call. There are such terms of endearment as:
"Hey, Droopy Drawers" or "Oh, Babbit Ass".
If my mate called me babbit ass, especially
in public, I'd trade him off for a new one.
My favorite was a couple who had been married
40 years, walking hand in hand, he still
called her "Princess" and she answered, "Yes,
love."
     As we rounded the corner towards the
middle of the show, the air was filled with
the sounds of shuffling feet, the constant
chatter of the Snowbird, and the aroma of
baking cinnamon rolls, roasting peanuts and
sizzling barbecue. We tried to move fast
through this area and act like we didn't
smell the enticing aroma, but my stomach
started doing flip flops and hollering for
attention. It was getting close to lunch
time. "I'm going to have an Indian taco.
Maybe I'll have some yogurt for dessert and
just one of those delicious cinnamon rolls.
Can I get anybody else anything?" I asked.
     "I thought we were going to watch our

diet this year and not try to eat everything we see," Cork said.   "Look at all those fat people eating Indian tacos."

That's my honey, always worrying about my figure. "You stand in the cinnamon roll line while I get a taco and try to notice how slim the people are in that line," I told him.

After we had lunch the guys were acting tired and found a place to sit down while we ventured on.   They were waiting patiently when an old man and old woman hobbled by, both of them using canes. The old man had a flashlight tied around his neck with a string. He saw Cork and John sitting there looking a little bedraggled and came over and shined the flashlight in their faces.   He said, "I've been looking for a couple of smart guys, I've worn out six sets of batteries and haven't found one yet."

The variety of items for sale was as different as the people that were selling. There were wind chimes make from sliced agate, genuine Indian beads, figurines carved from ironwood, rawhide strips for stringing beads, and everything to make your own jewelry. Turquoise was selling in different size chunks, or in handcrafted silver and turquoise jewelry. Wood carvers were busy carving gnomes and old fashioned Santa Clauses. You could buy macrame rope and make your own lawn chairs, or make your own design on a shirt with punch embroidery. There were colorful, artificial flower shops, cowboy boots for the whole family, southwest pottery, down home country crafts from the Ozark Mountains and merchants selling blankets, rugs, and leather bags from Mexico. A cartoonist from New Hampshire was selling RV greeting cards and family tee shirts especially made for campers. The tee shirts we're reasonably priced so I took time to stock up for the grandkids.

Antiques seemed to come from everywhere.
They ranged from old comic books, marbles and
toys, to dishes of all kinds. I ran into a
lady from Oregon who had been in Nebraska to
close out her aunt's estate. She had two
trailer loads of antique furniture and dishes
to get rid of. I lost whatever self control
I claimed to have earlier. I love the old
oak furniture and she had two oak rocking
chairs, a smaller one for grandma and the
bigger one for grandpa. My husband started
screaming like a scared raven. "You can't buy
that stuff, we don't have room to haul it!"

I've wanted a rocking chair ever since we
visited the Ozarks two years ago. All the
homes had rocking chairs on the front porch.
In the evenings they all sit on the porch
where it's cool just "relaxin" and a
"rockin." As we traveled the back roads of

Missouri, I said to my mate, "Why don't we
stop in a rocking chair place and buy me a
rocker? You can build a porch on the back of
the motorhome. That way I can sit on the
porch and rock while you're driving." He
just rolled his eyes and kept on trucking.

The very pleasant lady make me a deal I
couldn't refuse. Since we were cramped for
space I only bought the smaller one for me.
I wanted two old oak dressers, but decided I
really needed to remember where we were and
how much room I wanted to give up for these
treasures, so instead I bought several pieces
of Jewel Tea dishes in the autumn leaf
pattern. I started a collection several
years ago and still couldn't resist buying a
few to finish out my set. Every time I
thought my set was complete, I ran into
something I didn't know existed.

All the lady Snowbirds from our flock were collectors. Dee was collecting old cookie jars; Beryl kept her eyes out for Agatha Christie novels, and LaVern had a doll collection, small china tea sets and cups and saucers. It kept us busy watching for everybody's favorites, and with all of us looking, we didn't miss a thing.

In some circles Snowbirds are compared to the crow. They keep dragging shiny objects home to the nest. When the nest gets full they pack it on top. I surely didn't want my rocking chair on top of the motorhome. To start with, I needed to worry about how to get it back to the nest. "Too bad it won't fit in the pull cart," I said.

The male Snowbird is built somewhat like the Canadian goose. His neck is long so that he can stretch it over and above the crowd and spot his mate, wherever she may be. I never have to worry about getting lost because my mate always knows where I am, except when he senses I might need help to carry my purchases. Then, and only then, does he lower his neck and lose himself in the crowd.

I knew if I could find Bill he would come after the rocker in his pickup. Bill's the type of Snowbird that rises in the morning with nothing to do and has it all done by noon. If my guess is right he's already back at the nest having his afternoon nap.

We started working our way back towards the nest, dragging our cart and our tails, vowing to come back and finish this show another day. We were so tired we couldn't even remember where all the places were we had planned to return to. "They'll be there tomorrow," Beryl said.

When we reached camp, the rest of our flock from Nebraska had arrived and were chattering like a brood of magpies. Dick and Beverly, Waldo and Norma, and Ed and Margaret had their motorhomes pulled into the spaces reserved for them. Our flock of Snowbirds will be roosting in a circle this evening. In the morning we will move into the vee formation and spread out over the town, flying faster and functioning better now that our flock was nearly completed.

After hugs all around, the girls wanted to know what kind of bargains we had found that day. We took time for show and tell as each person showed her valuable purchases. Then I talked Bill into taking me for a ride in his pickup so I could "pick up" my rocker.

Later, as we were discussing what the flock was going to have for dinner, two more motorhomes stopped outside of our circle looking for the Nebraska flock. We welcomed Bob and Pat from Oregon and Don and Ellen from Wyoming. We all moved over and made room for more friends to join the circle. Bob and Pat would be staying to learn what boondocking was all about. Don and Ellen would only be with us one night. Boondocking didn't sound too exciting to them, instead they wanted to travel on to Phoenix and play golf on green grass. We tucked them under our wing for the evening and gathered them close like a mother goose.

That evening around the campfire was one of the most memorable experiences of the whole winter. Twenty-two of us sitting around the campfire relating the many stories about our RV travels, family life in different parts of the country, swapping fish tales, and planning the next day's activities. The most heart-wrenching story of all was Don and Ellen's account of their twenty-five year old daughter's fight for survival, then death, from the dreaded disease Leukemia.

Sensing a need to liven up the party, Will suggested we finish the evening with an old fashioned rousing square dance and sing-

along. We   have some very talented people in
our flock, and they dug out their instruments
and struck up a tune.   Bob played the guitar,
Pat   the   fiddle, and Waldo played the dobro.
Maxine and Dee   harmonized to   some   of   the
prettiest country western music   you ever did
hear.   They   were especially clever with, "If
You've Got The   Money   Honey,   I've   Got   The
Time.

John was the caller for the square   dance
as   he   shouted out the words and danced too,
"Here I come in   my   little red wagon, wheels
broke and the axle draggin'.   Allemande left
with   your   left   hand, partners right and a
right and left grand.   Meet ole' Sal and meet
ole' Sue, meet the gal that   came   with   you,
and   promenade two   by two.   Get em' on home
that's what you do."

Before we knew   what   had happened it was
12 o'clock.   The   lights were   out   in   the
motorhomes all   the   way around us.   We felt
lucky that boondocking Snowbirds didn't have
telephones or we would have   been   turned   in
long ago for disturbing the peace.   Bill made
his way to the   motorhome   and punched "Taps"
on his musical horn.

"I won't have to be rocked to sleep again
tonight," John said.

Chapter Five

WHAT'S FOR DINNER?

Before we arrive in Quartzsite everyone cooks up their own specialty. We each fix enough for a crowd. That way we don't have to spend all our valuable time preparing meals. John fixed a whopping pot of chili and a pot of beans. Beryl cooked two crockpots of beans, and I brought chili stew and enchiladas. Some of the others made big salads and brought hamburgers and steaks to cook out on the grill.

That first night John and Dee each made a pan of corn bread while Beryl warmed up the beans. My green chili stew came from Albuquerque, my sister-in-law's favorite recipe, but "hotter than Hades". It was delicious with the beans. "If I eat any more of that chili I'm going to have to go to the bathroom in the creek to keep from setting the desert on fire," John said.

We had several birthdays and anniversaries in our group so Beryl brought cake and ice cream to celebrate everyone's special days. I didn't think there was room in a motorhome freezer for ice cream, but Beryl found room. "The ice cream will cool down the chili," Beryl said. "When you're down at the creek tomorrow, John, all you have to do is holler 'come on ice cream,' that'll put the fire out."

The next day we all thawed out steaks and were talking about having baked potatoes to go with them. The guys offered to cook the steaks while we baked the potatoes in the microwave. It was nice having all the conveniences of home using the motorhome generator for electrical power. Norma and Margaret had ready made salads so dinner would be quite simple. Around the campfire the night before we started talking about baking the potatoes. The ironwood used in the campfire left coals burning all night. Usually by the next evening you could still light the campfire from the glowing coals.

"I don't see why we can't bake the potatoes in the coals from the fire," Maxine said. "If we're going to rough it, let's do it right."

"No, you won't ever get them done," Cork told her.

"Why don't we try it, they would be delicious?" Dee asked.

So Dee and Maxine fixed fifteen potatoes, wrapped them in foil and brought them outside and stirred them down into the coals from the night before. From the fireside gallery a long discussion evolved about how long it would take to cook potatoes. Some thought they better be checked every 30 minutes and could possibly be done on the first check.

"There's no way the potatoes will be done that soon, it will take at least an hour," Jeri said.

"Why don't you guys let an expert potato cooker take care of things," Maxine said. She came out to check them the first time and they were still hard as a rock. The second time was the same. After ninety minutes she pulled two potatoes from the coals and took them into her motorhome to take a closer look. The potatoes were burnt to a crisp. "We better warm up the beans again, the potatoes are cremated," she announced. From that time on John called Maxine our "little tater cooker."

After about three days of eating beans and Mexican food, the conversation around the campfire was bound to turn to the consequences of too many beans. "If we eat beans one more day I'm going to be floating. My feet never will touch the ground," Dick said.

"It's too bad we can't figure out a way to bottle this gas, recycle it and market it," Bill said. "We could set up a booth over here at Tyson's and make us a million dollars."

"O.K. we get the message," Norma said. "They sell everything else here, maybe we can find something to cure your problem while we're shopping tomorrow.

The next day as we dragged in after all day at the shows, LaVern was the first one to say she had found a solution to our growing gas problem. She had a wooden spoon for each couple. The spoons had a ladder for the handle. She said, "This is called a

boondocker's bean spoon. You put the spoon
in the beans while they're cooking and all
the little farts climb up the ladder and jump
over the side."

Dee and Maxine thought they had an idea
that would make us all some money. "We can
sack up bags of beans and set up a booth and
sell them for bath bubbles," Maxine said.

"If we don't do something soon we'll all
be known as the bean geese instead of
Snowbirds," I told them. "There really is
such a thing as a bean goose, I found it in a
book I'm reading," We all agreed the
solution to our problem was to have
hamburgers for supper the next night.

"Food tastes so good out here. I can't
tell if it's the good company we're keeping
or the great out of doors. Maybe it's just
the idea of eating someone else's cooking,"
Ed said.

We were enjoying the mild weather and
being able to eat dinner outside on the
picnic tables. The hard work we were doing

was producing an appetite like some of us had
never had before. We all knew we were in
trouble if we continued eating like fattened
hogs.

In the mornings we prepared breakfast in
our own motorhomes, usually a bowl of cereal.
We had a tendency to eat too much as we
wandered around the shows searching for a
bargain. Good food was around every corner.
Lunch started about 10 o'clock in the morning
and lasted until three in the afternoon, then
we went home and ate beans.

There was Indian fry bread, fried ice
cream, buffalo burgers, polish sausage,
yogurt, cinnamon rolls, honey roasted
almonds, hot dogs, funnel cakes, Chinese food
on a stick, curly fries, barbecue beef and
chicken and many, many more scrumptious
items.

Like the Canadian goose, the Snowbird
tends to be a heavy-bodied species. When
Snowbirds reach the age of 50 and beyond,
everything they eat starts developing into
what is known as the middle and lower body,
sometimes called middle-age spread. The
male, along with his long neck, sprouts a
large upper stomach while maintaining his
slim, skinny legs. The female bird adds to
her beauty by becoming more shapely. The
bosoms, the hips, stomach and legs rapidly
blossom into what is known as elegant
maturity.

My elegant maturity was getting out of
hand. "I think we should start some kind of
exercise program. Walking around the shows
doesn't give us a good enough workout to burn
off calories, or to get the heart pumping and
keep the cholesterol moving through the
arteries," I said.

"We need to do something," Beryl said.
"I always know when I'm getting too fat.
When I walk my butt flops up and hits me in
the back. I'm blossoming in the wrong

places."

Norma, Margaret, Bev, LaVern, Beryl and I all started a walking program in the evenings. Dee, Maxine, and Pat were too

tired after a long day shopping. They were skinny anyway and didn't need to watch their weight.

"Let's do the fast walk and pump our arms, like they do for the Olympics," Bev said.

"While you're doing that be sure to throw your shoulders back and suck in your stomach," Margaret added.

"In order to exercise the flabby part of your rear end, you should tighten the muscle on the left cheek when you step out with the right foot. Then do the same on the other side," LaVern said.

"Now, let me see if I have this all straight. We're holding our shoulders back while pumping our arms, sucking in our stomach, walking fast, and tucking in our cheeks one at a time. I didn't know walking had to be so much work," I said, as we huffed and puffed our way around the desert.

"We can call this the Suck and Tuck Snowbird Strut," Norma said, "but be careful you don't throw your back out." As we rounded the corner by our motorhomes, we heard a few giggles and smart remarks.

"From the back it looks like a bunch of kids fightin' under a blanket," Dick said, "Ha! Ha! Ha!" At least six other eerie cackles could be heard in the background.

"It wouldn't hurt you guys to get a little exercise too. You're more apt to have a heart attack than we are. At least we'll be in shape to go out looking for a new gander after you croak from cackling and eating," Beryl told them.

"There isn't a better place to start looking than right here. It's Snowbird Mating Season," Norma said.

Later that evening as we started playing bridge, we discussed what else we could do to get in the mood for losing weight. "When we shop in Yuma next week we can try on bikini bathing suits," Beverly suggested. "That always encourages me to diet."

"I'm not trying on a bikini," Margaret said. "If I ever wiggled into one they'd charge me for it because I wouldn't be able to find it."

"I heard on TV that a more curvacious body is in for the 90s. You can wear your skirts from the 60s, your underwear in public and eat all you want. So, the way I see it anything goes. I'll just buy a bigger size," LaVern said.

I knew I was going to have to do something drastic. Last year when we returned from our vacation, my friend Jerra called and said, "We knew you'd look like a blimp when you came home, so we signed you up on our team for the weight loss contest.

"I don't know how you knew, but you're right," I answered. "I'm miserable. I gained so much weight I had to wear sweat pants all the way home. I can't get into any of my clothes."

"So what are you going to wear to church tomorrow?" she asked.

"Maybe if I wear a bright colored blouse nobody will notice I have on my sweat pants," I answered meekly.

She hesitated a minute, then added, "Weigh-in is at 4 o'clock on Monday."

I was determined that I wouldn't go home looking like that again this year. It takes all summer to wear it off. I made up my mind I was going to use my will power, do the Snowbird Strut, and watch everything I put in my mouth.

The next day while walking around Cloud's Jamboree we ran into a vendor who gave us a recipe for elephant stew. "Let's try this on the guys and see how they like it," Maxine said.

"It looks like it will serve enough people. We could advertise it in the paper and invite all the Snowbirds in our corner of the desert and still have food left over," Dee said.

"O.K. let's do it. I'll make the cake," Norma said.

ELEPHANT STEW

1 elephant	2 rabbits
salt and pepper	clove of garlic

Cut elephant into bite size pieces. Salt and pepper. Cover all with brown gravy. Cook over kerosine fire about four weeks at 465 degrees. This will serve 3,800 people. If more are expected, add the two rabbits. Do this only in an emergency however, as most

people do not like hare in their stew.   To
complete the menu serve the following recipe
for Clearwater Rum Cake.   Author unknown.

CLEARWATER RUM CAKE

1 or 2 qts. rum   1 cup butter
1 tsp. sugar   2 large eggs
2 cups dried fruit   baking powder

    Before you start, sample the rum to check
the quality. Good isn't it?   Now go ahead
and select a large mixing bowl, measuring
cup, etc. Check the rum again. It must be
just right. To be sure rum is of highest
quality, pour 1 level cup of rum into a glass
and drink it as fast as you can. Repeat.
With an electric mixer, beat 1 cup butter in
a large fluffy bowl.   Add one seaspoon of
tugar and beat again.   Meanwhile, make sure
the rum is of the finest quality.   tri
another cup. Open second quart if necessary.
Add 2 arge leggs, 2 cups fried druit and beat
until high.   If the druit gets stuck in the
beaters, just pry it loose with a
drewscriber. Sample the rum again, checking
for toncisticity. Next sift 3 cupd baking
powder, a pinch of rum, a seaspoon of toda, a
cup of pepper or salt (It really ddoesn't
matter0 sample rum again.   Sift one half
pint lemon juice. Fold in chopped butter and
strained nuts.   Add 1 shaglespoon of brown
tuger, or whatever color you can find. Wix
mel. Grease oven and set cake pan for 350
degrees. Now pour the whole mess into the
oven.   Maybe it would be better to forget the
coven and the ake. Just check the rum again
and bo to ged.

Author unknown.

Chapter Six

PRESERVING WATER

"Singing in the rain, just singing in the
rain," I was singing in the shower,
thoroughly enjoying myself. Although our
little shower was somewhat of a problem for
my over-weight body. Or maybe it was my body
that was a burden to the narrow shower. Each
time I moved or tried to bend over to wash my

feet, or other down low parts of the body, I bumped into the sides, bonking my head.

I was washing my hair and had just put the shampoo on for the second time when the water quit. We had been here two days and this was my first shower. Walking around at the shows was dirty business. It hadn't rained for weeks and the dust on the roadway where we walked to and from Tyson's show was covered with three inches of powdered dirt. I have no idea how people last for a week without a shower. I went without a shower yesterday and had to have one today.

Beryl had mentioned the night before that water preservation was very important to the male Snowbird. I hadn't asked her what she meant by that, but I was about to find out. My mate was outside standing around last night's campfire drinking coffee with the other guys. They were taking bets as to whose wife would be the last one ready to go that morning. My husband had just finished telling them that he knew I would be the last one ready. "She is always last," he said.

I don't know how he expects me to be ready any sooner. He always takes over the bathroom first in the mornings and I have to wait for him to finish before I can even start getting ready. As small as this bathroom is I suppose I could sit on the pot while brushing my teeth with one hand and shaving my legs with the other. I hollered out the vent in the shower, "Cork, somebody turned off the water, come in here and turn it back on."

He took his time while I was standing there soap dripping in my eyes and shivering in the cool morning air. He pushed the button on the wall that tells you how much water is left in the tank, and it registered empty. "Nobody turned the water off. You used it all," he said.

"You told me we had a big water tank, we

can't be out of water yet," I answered. I had only been in the shower for 20 minutes, there wasn't any way I had used up all the water. "What am I supposed to do with a head full of shampoo? Go see if someone will loan us a bucket of water so I can get this shampoo out of my hair."

It was plain to see I had a lot to learn about motorhome living and camping. The night before I had washed dishes letting the water run the whole time for rinsing. I had also cleaned and washed some raw vegetables, leaving the water run. I didn't realize there was any other way to wash dishes or vegetables.

By the time I had my hair rinsed and the generator turned on so I could dry my hair and curl it with the curling iron, everybody else was ready to leave for the Main Event.

"We can't stand around here all day waiting for you to primp, you're the last one to get ready," my husband added, as patiently as any husband would in a situation like this.

That evening, while we were fixing supper I received my education about water preservation. Beryl and LaVern were giving free instructions. Beryl said, "We just wash dishes once a day, after supper. We take turns bringing dish water out to the picnic tables. We have a community dish washing party. If we take turns furnishing water then it will last a week. After a week we travel into town and refill and dump the sewer. They both should last a week if we are careful."

LaVern said, "If you're careful when taking a shower you won't use much water. You turn the water on and get wet all over, then you turn it off while you soap down, and back on to rinse. And you're only allowed one shower a week. The rest of the time you take a finger bowl bath."

    "Next you're going to tell me I have to
shower with a friend. Who ever heard of
taking a finger bowl bath? That bathroom
sink looks like a finger bowl. If we have to
do community dish washing maybe we should
have a community shower, too," I suggested.
"We can put a 50 gallon barrel of water on
top of one of the motorhomes and let the sun
heat it. We used to do that when we had
outdoor toilets,"
    They went on telling me all the do's and
don'ts. "Never leave water running anytime,
for dishes, vegetables or anything else. You
also have to learn to use a small amount in
the toilet," LaVern said.

SAVE
WATER
SHOWER
WITH A
FRIEND!

"Holy cow, next you'll be telling me I can't go to the pot either. I suppose I'll have to go to the bathroom in the creek like John," I said. I knew camping wasn't any fun. I can't believe anyone goes a week without a bath. It's not sanitary."

"There is no creek, that's why we have to preserve water, Beryl said. "Water is a precious commodity in the desert. The male Snowbird doesn't like to move his rig any oftener than he has to. The main reason is because you can waste half a day waiting in line to fill up again. If you want to see an unhappy Snowbird, tell him every morning his rig is out of water. The feathers start flying and he squawks like a chicken with his head cut off."

I noticed they had porta-potties at the shows. "I'm surprised they haven't figured out they can charge a fee for using the toilets. They can charge like they do in China where people don't have bathrooms in their homes. Men are allowed to use the public toilets free, but women are charged a fee equal to two cents," I said. "We could get into a long discussion about why that is, but evidently the women's liberation movement hasn't arrived in China yet."

We were washing dishes that evening when we heard a musical horn playing. It sounded like the old ice cream wagons that used to run up and down the street many years ago. "If that's an ice cream wagon, I'll take a double dip of butter pecan," I hollered at my mate.

"It's the honey bucket," Bill said.

"I don't need any honey, what are honey buckets for?" I asked. "I had my mouth all set for an ice cream cone."

"Cork, you better hail him down. If you ran out of water today that means your sewer is full," Bill told him. "The honey bucket is a truck with a tank on it that pumps out

your sewer. Sometimes it's much easier to
have them pump it than wait in line at one of
the dumps."

Cork had them stop and pump out our
sewer. Nobody else in our flock needed
theirs pumped out. "I don't know how you can
stand the stink of leaving the sewer sit for
a week either. Doesn't it get pretty rank in
this small place and as warm as it is?" I
asked.

"Not if you use the chemical you bought
yesterday. Come on I'll show you how much to
use," Beryl said. "It's against BLM rules
and regulations to dump any water on the
ground. Most self-contained vehicles have a
grey water holding tank and a black water
holding tank. There are Snowbirds who think
they can get away with dumping their grey
water on the ground. Grey water is that
which is used in the shower and sinks. Water
used for the toilet is black water. It's
important that everyone abides by the rules
if they expect to have a place for campers on
BLM land," Beryl continued.

The next day it rained. The women were
running around putting buckets under the
awning so they could catch the water. I
started asking questions again like a three
year old. "Now what are you doing?" I asked.
This is where I learned a valuable lesson.

"We use the water to wash our hair, rain
water is extra soft and is very good for hair
washing," Beverly told me.

I made a bee-line for my bucket,
hollering at my husband all the way. "Let
one side of the awning down so the water will
run into my bucket," I said. I knew there
was some reason for buying that awning. I
salvaged enough water that day to wash my
hair two more times.

When we crawled into bed that night, we
discovered that the bed was wet. Rain had
leaked in around the air conditioner. It

soaked the foam mattress and was a mess.
"Now what do we do?" I asked.

"Well, we wanted to know what kind of bed the dinette makes, now's our chance to find out," Cork said.   To my surprise it made a very good bed, small but comfortable.   One thing for sure, there wasn't any room for flopping around.

The next day all the bedding had to be put outside to dry.   Some of the neighbors were looking at us like maybe we had wet the bed.   "Don't look at me," I said.   "I didn't wet the bed.   I'm afraid to drink any water for fear we'll run out.   I'm so dry I can't even spit."

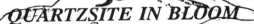

QUARTZSITE IN BLOOM

Let Me go to Quartzite
Afore I die!
Where the Mountains
and the Valley
Come up to meet the sky.

There people come from miles
around
To sell their wares
In this Desert town
Where 20th Century Prospectors
Are looking for the Mother lode
The place where Hi Jolly
Once on a camel rode.

Old and bowed figures
Changed the landscape
With their spades
And men with calloused hands
Run the diggins in the Caves.

The natives are seen to smile
At the economy boost
When the Wintering Snowbirds
Fly down here to roost.

Tables and Tents
On four sides of town
RV's and Hookups
All over the ground.

One's a hawkin rocks
Another selling shades
Some a sackin fruits
Others makin Trades

If you Choose to see Tyson Wells
Or stop at the Main Event
Shop with a Tail gater
Or buy rocks under a tent.

This is the place to be
To Buy antiques and gems and such
If you miss this crossroads
gathering
You've missed so very much.

For Quartzsite and it's character
Is like a desert's bloom
Disappears most of the year.
Then becomes ten thousand rooms!

Chapter Seven

THE MAIN EVENT

The water problems were all solved and the female Snowbirds were all preened and ready to go for the day. We all piled into the back of Bill's pickup and started our journey to the west end of town to the Main Event. Everyone gathered up their trash to dump in a trailer near the entrance of the parking area.

The Snowbirds were out in droves on a cloudy overcast morning. We waited patiently for our turn to pull onto Highway 95 from our camping area. A new four way stop had been installed on the south side of the bridge and traffic moved slowly but smoothly. As we inched our way over the bridge, I decided to climb out and take a few pictures. I had plenty of time. No one at home will ever believe this without pictures.

As we turned left at the intersection on Business 10 and started west, we were behind a faded yellow school bus with a porch built on the back. An old wringer washing machine sat on the porch standing guard. I wondered where they found enough water to run the antique. Torn, faded curtains fluttered through the dirty open windows, with bare-footed, dirty-faced kids staring out at the $100,000 RV bus passing beside them. A sign on the old bus's door read, "Poverty Flats".

We stopped at the post office to buy stamps and saw an interesting sight, a smelly billy goat was tied to the mail drop. As we glanced over towards Interstate 10 there appeared a covered wagon pulled by a tractor, with a whole family of settlers looking for a place to settle. Over to the south of the Interstate was another interesting sight. A restaruant called the Airport Garden's Dinner House, with a small airplane camped on the roof. Maybe someone just stopped in for dinner. They say you can see everything in Quartzsite, now I believe it.

The Main Event Gemboree was kicked off this year by the History of Quartzsite Pageant. It was held at the Main Event Arena on January 11 and 12. The Main Event itself got underway on January 19 and was to run through February 3rd.

"Next year we're going to have to come earlier, we're missing out on a lot of fun. I know I would enjoy the Pageant and look at all the other neat things they have going on," I said. Opening day featured hot air balloons, an Antique & Classic car show, Mexicali Folk Dancers, skydiving performances, a professional rodeo, an old timer's rodeo, camel races, aerial fireworks and a country western show featuring the Reinsmen in the Big Top Tent.

The word was out, Mayor Richard Oldham participated in the camel races and had a bad fall. It's a long way to the ground from the top of a camel. He was in the hospital in Parker with three broken ribs and a broken shoulder blade. Mayor Oldham said, "Two years riding in this event is enough, I won't ride again next year."

The Main Event is open year around and has several dealers and vendors who maintain their booths all year. The headquarters of the Main Event houses a grocery store, U.S. Post Office, restaurant, barber shop and laundromat. The building is decorated as a sort of Gothic cathedral of wood. Beams which support the ceiling protrude around the eaves of the building and are carved into figures. Jim Freeman, a wood carver from Oregon, is the sculptor. Jim arrives each year in time for the celebration and carves throughout the show. The ends of the beams form different animals. A giraffe's head forms one end of the beam, while on the other side of the wall is its tail. The building contains a wall of solid agate, a "Fool's gold" wall and a quartz ore wall. A model of a mine has been built outside featuring a train line through the mountains between the mine and the smelter.

Inside the headquarters there's a 1915 Model T that had served as an ice cream truck in Seattle, Washington. There is a mural that presents scenes from one coast of the United States to another, starting with the Washington coastline and ending with New York City. Howard Armstrong is planning to extend the mural to include the entire world. On one counter is a gigantic amethyst crystal conglomeration. Its estimated worth is $6,000.

Many top name entertainers have performed at the Main Event Arena: Roy Clark, Hank Thompson, Richard Snow and the Snowflakes, The Bob Wills Band, The San Antone Rose Band, David Givens, The Murphy Family, Barbara Mandrell and Dave Salyer, and many more.

As we pulled into the dusty parking lot, we could see that many motorhomes had chosen to park in the area north of the Main Event grounds. After further investigation we found that parking is free, and you can stay as long as you like. There are about 1000 spaces reserved for vendors. The vendors can park motorhomes or trailers in their rented space, complete with electricity and water. The honey bucket comes around regularly for sewer dumping for a charge of $5.

As we walked into the vending area, the

sounds of country music filled the air as an overweight Johnny Gatlin was singing to taped music. We stood and listened for a short time, then moved on. There were different entertainers performing all over the show grounds. It wasn't long until the men were looking for a place to rest.

"Here's a good place for you to rest," Norma said to Waldo. A rodeo bull rider brought one of his favorite bulls with him and was taking pictures of anyone brave enough to climb on.

"That bull's as tired and as old as I am, he doesn't have enough energy left to buck anyone off," Waldo said. He walked by, gave the aged bull a pat, and continued on his way.

As we rounded the corner on the front row along Business 10, we heard the drone of a man spouting poetry over a small loudspeaker. We stopped to listen to the rambling voice coming from a kind man with grey hair, a formed-to-fit felt hat and a generous smile. The poetry flowed like honey from his mouth as he recited poem after poem about people at play, at work and at home. Some were written for humor, some written for the heart. T.J Finley was selling his poems on postcards or 8x10 prints. His wife was selling homemade crafts and beautiful Indian dolls. They also had some gorgeous Alpaca wall hangings and rugs made from the llama.

T.J. and his lovely wife are from Cordell, Oklahoma. He reminded me of a farmer, as his rough, calloused hands indicated that he had been a hard working man. T.J. is retired now and he and his wife have discovered the magic that draws snowbirds to the Arizona desert. They spend the summer months preparing for their trip back to Quartzsite each winter to sell their wares. They are Snowbird vendors from December 12 to the middle of February.

    T.J. gave me   permission to print two of
his poems in this book.   He has many others
to choose from, such as "Home At Last" and
"Wave On".   He has a new one named "The
Vendor's Prayer".   Be sure and stop at the
Main Event and talk to T.J. Finley and listen
as he recites poetry.
    Wandering on around the corner, the aroma
of sizzling onions   on a buffalo burger
started my mouth drooling as the hunger pangs
sprung into action.   So far this morning I
had only eaten one sack of honey roasted
almonds. "I'm having withdrawal pains from

yogurt. Shall we all have a large cone?" I asked.

"I'm not eating," came the reply from six people at the same time. I had to eat a cone all by myself. I think they planned the whole thing to make me feel guilty, as I continued to watch everything I put in my mouth.

As we were strolling along we ran into Gary and Evelyn Buchanan, a couple from Scappoose, Oregon. Our attention was drawn to them by the sassy looking tee shirts they were wearing.

Gary works for the fire department in Portland. They were on vacation, staying in an RV, doing some short time boondocking.

Dee and Maxine were at the height of their glory at the Main Event. There was booth after booth of antique dishes. Dee gathered up five old cookie jars and had three more spotted to come back for another time. Maxine was busy bartering for more Frankhoma Pottery. She said, "I'll wait a few days and come back, they'll lower their price just before the end of the show."

"These two women have junk spotted all over town that they want to come back and purchase later. I have one man that wants me to rent his trailer to haul it all home in. If they don't quit buying we'll never get back to Northern California. We'll have to set up shop right here," Jeri said.

We all bought a cutting board made from Corian. The man selling them cut the boards to any size. Every motorhome has different size sink openings and the boards will fit right into the sink or can be cut for any other need. My motorhome had an opening in the kitchen countertop for a small trash receptacle. I didn't like it there so bought a Corian cutting board to fill the space. Living in the wilderness like we do in Nebraska, we have to travel quite a ways to find ready made items for motorhomes. So Quartzsite is a place where we stock up on everything we'll need for another year. And maybe just a few things we don't really need.

The vendors are all friendly people and I decided I wanted to talk with some of them to see where they came from and how long they had beem coming here. I visited with Anna Mae and Red Brown who had loads of antiques. They had some beautiful old dishes, one of my weaknesses. They are located in Tucson and travel around to antique shows. They have been coming to the Main Event for nine years. "We've sold a lot this year," Red said, "although this could be our last year because I have cancer of the throat. I have to think positive and have confidence that I will still be around to come another year."

I had an interesting visit with Jo Gavin from Jackson, Wyoming. She was selling Western jackets, American Indian jewelry, Frankhoma pottery and other collectibles. The name of her booth was Jo's Metal Wigwam. Jo has been RVing full time for six years. She said, "My kids thought I was crazy to even think about RVing by myself after my husband died." She travels with her watch dog. I didn't think he looked too fierce, but she warned me not to get too close. "He's saved my life several times," she said. Jo went on to say, "I could write my own book about my travels if I'd take time to sit down and do it. I took a picture of her and her booth but this generic snowbird walked in front of my camera.

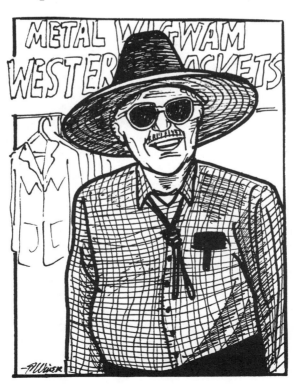

Jo said, "It has paid well for me to belong to the Good Sam Emergency Road Service. The first two years I was on the road I had to be towed in eight times." The Good Sam Club is a special club just for RV'ers of all kinds. Jo told of traveling behind a motorhome going down the road when their awning started rolling in and out. Before they could stop the awning was all twisted to pieces. Then she said she was traveling behind another motorhome when the sewer connection broke. "The whole front end of my motorhome was covered with crap and I had to stop and clean it off. I got sick to my stomach. Thank God that doesn't happen too often."

After taking in the model airplane show, watching the kids at the petting zoo, and listening to two other entertainers, the guys started looking bored and tired, so we decided maybe we should call it a day and head back to the nest. We wanted to be in top form tomorrow to take in the Pow Wow, the Four Corners area, and the Sports Vacation and RV show at the big tent.

We made a stop at the grocery store for bread, milk and mostly to pick up a lottery ticket. At the grocery store there was a couple of entertainers playing the guitar and singing, hoping to pick up some tips between performances at the Main Event or other shows.

The Arizona Lottery jackpot was sitting at $21 million. The odds in winning the Pick's jackpot are one in 5.2 million. Now that we had those facts we all stepped up to the window to purchase our tickets. My husband, the last of the big spenders, stepped up to the window first. "I'm only going to buy $2 worth," he said. John purchased $5 worth of tickets and some of the ladies bought $3 worth. Beryl didn't buy.

"I've got to have at least $10.00 worth," Eddie said. "Your chances of winning increase with every dollar's worth you buy."

Waldo, the high roller in our group, stepped right up and ordered $25 worth. Some of the other guys bought $5 and $10 worth. Norma, Beverly and I were studying the odds and trying to figure out how we could pick the right numbers to win the big bucks. "Let's pick our own numbers instead of taking the quick pick," Bev said.

"Let's see, if we pool our money, pick our own numbers, and spend $10 apiece it will raise the odds. Which will almost guarantee us a winner of some kind," I added.

"O.K. that sounds like a winner, but it will take us forever to pick out that many numbers, I don't think the guys will stand around and wait for us that long. We'll have to go with the Quick Pick at least for part of them," Norma said. It was plain to see we weren't used to buying lottery tickets. We finally arrived at a decision and put Norma in charge of buying the tickets. Now all we had to do was wait till 10 o'clock, turn on the TV, and have our celebration when they called out our numbers. There's really nothing to this game.

On the way home, riding in the back of Bill's pickup, letting the wind blow our hair, watching the crazy Snowbirds coming and going like ants around an ant hill, I started thinking about how rich we already are. Maybe we don't have a million dollars, but we are rich in many other ways. Why would anyone ever need any more than what we already have? Thinking about winning millions of dollars makes people go crazy. Every night sitting around the campfire, gazing at the stars and the moon on a still night, has often times brought on these words from someone in our group, "I wonder what the poor people are doing tonight?"

That evening we were all anxiously waiting the big drawing for the lottery. As you may have guessed we never won a dime off of the Arizona shysters. The Arizona Lottery has so much money that they have to draw twice a week. So twice a week crazy Snowbirds stop off at the grocery store and spend thousands of dollars, while many people all over the world are going hungry. The big winners of the lottery are the insurance companies, says E.J. Montini a columnist for the Arizona Republic. The winner receives $1 million dollars a year for the next 21 years. The state takes their 50% off the top and the insurance companies rake in the money from the interest. I hope the insurance companies donate once in a while to the poor and needy people. What a deal! From now on I'm only buying a $2.00 ticket.

Chapter Eight

STORIES AROUND THE CAMPFIRE

The best part of the day was the evening after the dishes were all washed. We all pulled our lawn chairs into a circle around the dancing flames of the ironwood campfire. We'd listen to the snap and crackle of the fire and gaze in wonder at the moon and stars on a balmy, bright winter evening.

The people in our flock were from all different walks of life and different parts of the country, but the one thing we had in common was a love for the RV way of life. The many and varied stories that were told about our escapades around the country took up the bulk of our evenings as we all took turns spinning yarns, relating stories about our travels and telling lies about who caught the biggest fish.

Bill and Beryl and John and LaVern had been doing more traveling than the rest of us and had more experiences with their RV. When Bill and Beryl eagerly left the Nebraska cold country, they were driving a new Foretravel, a top of the line motorhome. "The first three months we had that thing we spent more time sitting along the road than we ever have since. We sold it a few years ago and bought a used Executive. I'm sure we had all the kinks worked out and I imagine the people who have it now think it's wonderful," Beryl said.

"We really had an experience last summer," Bill said, "We were getting ready to go to Alpine, Arizona, to get out of the heat. The day before we left home, I had taken the motorhome to town to fill up with butane and blew out a tire. I bought a new one, had it mounted and thought we were ready to travel. We were five miles west of Tucson when the motor suddenly died. I could see the waves of heat rising off the pavement, and took my life in my hands as the traffic on the Interstate went zooming by. I opened up the battery compartment to see what had gone wrong this time and found that the batteries had slid together and shorted out. After getting that fixed we were back on the road again when about a mile east of Tucson we blew another tire, so back to Tucson where we had trouble finding motorhome tires. It took all day but we finally found one and had it mounted. They assured us they had 10 tires on order. The next day, back on the road again ten miles out of Wilcox, Arizona, we blew the third tire. We thought we could find a tire in Wilcox, but there were no motorhome tires in town. We called back to Tucson and told them we needed four more new tires. Much to our surprise the Tire Shop had received their order. We stayed all night in Wilcox, then drove into Tucson on five tires. We replaced the four remaining tires, each one costing forty dollars more than the one we bought in Yuma. It ended up costing us $1000 for tires."

"We learned the hard way that there is a reason why you see most motorhomes with their tires covered in this ghastly heat. If you don't want to buy new tires every year you better keep the sun away from them. You also need to keep the dash covered or it will burn up, crack, and peel in the hot sun. We didn't think anything else could possibly go wrong, but when driving over the pass near Mule Creek, New Mexico, we blew a radiator hose. It's always a good idea to have an extra radiator hose too," Bill said.

Bill continued, "We were beginning to think we had the old Foretravel back. But, I guess if you don't take care of your vehicles it doesn't matter what kind you have. We were trying to run away from the heat, but for some reason or other, we weren't getting the job accomplished. For a short time I was even thinking maybe Nebraska winters weren't so bad after all."

"Was anyone knocking on our door last night?" LaVern wanted to know. "I kept hearing a knocking sound, and when I went to the door no one was there."

"It was probably a kangaroo rat," Beryl said.

"What are kangaroo rats?" LaVern asked.

"When you look around in the desert you

can see their holes under the greasewood bushes. They can jump four feet high and squeeze through a small hole. If you don't want them to get in your motorhome you better use some insect spray around the wheel wells and anyplace else they might get in," Beryl said, "And when you hear them knocking don't let them in!"

"This is a good time to tell us I won't be able to sleep tonight for worrying about rats climbing in bed with me," LaVern said. "Are you saying they can jump up and knock on the door to be let in? If that's true I let four of them in last night. That's how many times I opened the door."

Let me tell you about our experience with mice in the motorhome," Beryl said. "We were camping in a State Park up by Gunnison, Colorado. Bill parked us by three garbage cans. I kept telling him we had mice in the motorhome, but he thought I was hearing things again. We opened the bathroom door and looked in the shower and one of the nasty little critters was sitting up looking at us. The next day we could hear them running between the walls in the shower. Gus, our dog, was having a big time playing with the mice."

"I heard them announcing on the radio that morning to beware of mice trying to move inside because of the cold weather coming on. We went into town and bought all the mouse traps they had. I could smell mouse pee everywhere. I ran around pouring vinegar everywhere I knew they had been. Gus and Bill chased one up under the hood, Bill couldn't get at him so he swatted him with the fly swatter, then sprayed him with fly spray. He came running out and our friend Charlie whopped him with his hand and killed him. We caught eight mice in five days. Gus really was enjoying those mice, he thought they were part of the family."

Beryl continued, "From then on every time we went any place we got mice in the motorhome. Whenever we went out to the desert, rock or coin hunting, we'd get a kangaroo rat. The kangaroo rat doesn't drink water so you can't use D-Con on them. The larger rat is fourteen inches long and yellowish tan in color. There is a smaller species that is eight to ten inches long, they are a yellowish color too, but have a white stripe on their tail. The crazy things got into Gus's food and carried it all over the motorhome. I opened the glove compartment where Bill kept his gum and they had eaten two packages. Bill stuffed steel

wool in every crack he could find, but they
still got in. He finally found a place up
under the dash and since he filled it with
steel wool we haven't had any trouble."

"Somebody told me to put moth balls in
the motorhome and the mice wouldn't come in.
So I put a whole box around all over the
motorhome. We went from the mountains down
to Kimball to visit. When we arrived I went
out to the Country Club where I knew the
girls were playing golf. Bernita said she
could smell me coming. All my clothes
smelled like moth balls. The next day I hung
all of our clothes outside to air out," Beryl
added.

"Seems like we have to learn everything
the hard way," Bill said. "We don't park by
garbage cans anymore. Beryl scrubbed and
cleaned that motorhome until there wasn't
anything left to scrub, but she could still
smell mice. We finally bought new carpet and
had the seats upholstered, trying to get rid
of the smell. Mice can do a lot of damage to
a motorhome, so keep your cracks stuffed full
and keep D-Con around when your camper is
stored for a few months."

"If I ever see one of those rats in my
house I'll bail out and never go back in
again," Beverly said.

"I hate mice worse than anything else I
can think of, but if I saw a rat I'd probably
faint away and die of shock," I said.

"I've just the thing for you girls,"
Beryl said. She brought each of us a cute
little crocheted mouse with a dress on. It
had a string so it could be hung on the rear-
view mirror. "This will keep the mice away.
I haven't had any since I hung mine up."

"I wish you would look at the sky, I've
never seen a more awesome sight," John said.
"Who would ever think that we'd be sitting
out under the stars, looking at a full moon
the first of February? At home we'd get our

nose frost bitten if we stuck it outside the door. I wonder what the poor people are doing tonight."

"The poor people are the ones in Iraq and Kuwait that are hiding from the guns of war, and a leader that has gone berserk. Just think what it would be like to be one of them. God has truly blessed us with more than we need, but right now all we can do is support our troops and pray," I said.

"Have you ever seen a meteor shower?" Bill wanted to know. "One time when we were parked out in the desert alone, I was up in the middle of the night when off to the north the sky lit up in a shower of stars. It was truly an astounding sight.   I don't think there will be any more until spring, but if you stay around until April or May, you can see one then. They happen anywhere from two to four in the morning though."

"Count me out, I can't get up that early. It would have to be spectacular to get me out of bed at that hour," Maxine said.

"We should go out to Mesa RV sales on the east side of town and see if they have a motorhome John could buy," Cork said.

"John's already bought all the motorhome he's going to get," LaVern said. "Trading that last one in just about ruined me on ever buying another one. I liked my mini-home and if it would have had a bed anyplace except over the cab, we'd have kept it. We went over to Mesa, Arizona, to trade and had the mini-home pulled up beside the new one so we could unload it, and there were people coming in there to look at ours before we were moved out."

"LaVern was pouting and growling because I was just hauling stuff in the new one and dumping it. I'd already had 1/2 quart of Jim Beam," John said.

"Did that make you mad?" Eddie asked.

"No, it made me drunk," John answered.

"It bothered John so much he laid down and went to sleep. John gave up drinking after that, because when I was ready I just pulled that new motorhome out of there and found us a campground. It drove pretty good, I didn't think I did too bad for not having driven a motorhome before," LaVern said. "You never saw a more surprised look on anybody's face than on John's when he woke up."

"I told her I had a few more things I wanted to do in this lifetime. As soon as I get them done I'll go back and lay down on the bed and then she can drive. In the meantime I don't want her driving," John said.

"It's the best thing I ever found to get a man to quit drinking. If anyone needs my instructions, I give them out free," LaVern said.

"It's sad how there are some people in every group that have to ruin things for others," Waldo said. "We pulled in behind a trailer and a motorhome the other day when we were waiting to dump our sewer. I watched as both of them drove up close to the drain and turned their sewer loose without a hose. What an ugly mess, I almost couldn't get out and dump mine it stunk so bad. It's too bad they don't take a few minutes to learn how to operate all parts of an RV before they take it out on the road."

"The state has closed many of the sewer dumps that used to be in rest areas in Arizona because people don't know how to use them. They don't seem to care about property that doesn't belong to them, and they ruin it for those of us that do care," Bill said.

"I had an uncle that came to visit us from Oklahoma one time. He was pulling a little trailer. The first thing he wanted to know when he came in the house was where our sewer dump was. I told him we didn't have a dump and told him where there was a gas station downtown that had a dump he could use. I didn't pay much attention to what he was doing until I met him on the stairs. Here he came with a bucket of sewer carrying it in my house to dump downstairs in the toilet. I started gagging and almost threw up right there. He emptied his whole holding tank that way," LaVern said. "I smelled that gunk for a month.

"This is our 15th winter in Arizona and California. Sometimes I think it would be nice just to stay at home one winter, but then I get to thinking that some day we aren't going to be able to go at all. Then we can sit at home by the fire instead of out here in the desert," John said.

"There are many old people at Yuma that don't have any business being there. One couple we know has been coming to Yuma for years. Two years ago he had a stroke and hasn't been able to drive, and he can't talk. I try to make conversation, but he gets frustrated when I don't understand him. Her brother pulled the trailer up here for them last year, then went back home. This year her brother drove them to Yuma again. The next day they woke up to find the brother had died of a heart attack. It was really sad," Bill said.

"Many people have heart attacks or other major illnesses and then they're too sick to be moved home," Beryl said. "The ambulances are running day and night trying to keep up with the calls. There are a lot of things Snowbirds don't think about when they're ready to retire. When they change their place of residence, they have to start over with a new doctor, dentist, banker, and insurance agent. When their health starts failing it's time to stay home where they can be familiar with their own doctor and have their family close by to help them."

Beryl continued her story, "Here again Snowbirds are like the Canadian geese, they keep company with their fallen. When the goose is injured, the mate will stay behind and protect her until she is healed and ready to fly. By that time the rest of the flock is already gone and it isn't as easy for them to fly by themselves. Geese fly much faster and easier in flocks and in formation. They are constantly changing so the lead bird doesn't get tired. The birds behind are always honking encouragement to the lead goose."

"That just goes to prove if you're not the lead bird the scenery never changes, and if you're not able to fly with the big Snowbirds, stay on the ground," John added.

Beryl continued after being interrupted, "Most of the time injured geese have to stay until their flock returns the next year. Sometimes a whole family of geese will halt their migration to stay behind. If you ever notice Canadian geese with a flock of tame geese, it's probably because they have been tamed or left behind because of injury. The same thing happens to injured Snowbirds. They find themselves in a strange place, not knowing their doctor or knowing when they will be able to travel home."

"This is a good place to pick up used motorhomes or trailers. If a Snowbird dies his mate is always anxious to sell so she can go home. There are lots of bargains just hanging around waiting to be snatched up," Bill said.

"Did you ever get rid of your fleas Beryl?" Cork asked.

"No! That's another sad story. We were parked out in the desert doing some coin hunting when Gus chased an old jackrabbit. He caught him and was having quite a time playing with him. I finally made him leave the rabbit alone, but it was too late. Gus

started scratching and itching right away.
It wasn't too long after that I started
itching and scratching too. When we got home
I bathed Gus and put flea powder all over
him, then I bathed myself. Gus's fleas went
away, but I couldn't get rid of mine. I
think it was a mite of some kind. I couldn't
see them, but I was broken out all over, and
they were driving me crazy. We vacuumed the
house every day and sprayed flea spray
everywhere. I finally called the fumigators
and had them spray the whole house and the
motorhome. I even considered letting them
spray me. Weelll, noow! It wasn't funny,
they were biting me. Bill was making fun of
me and the fumigator thought I had lost it.
I don't care, we kept vacuuming and after
three months they finally quit biting me."
    "Why do you go coin hunting in the middle
of the desert?" Waldo asked.
    "We find the old army bases. This
country is full of old World War II Army
bases. Bouse, Arizona, was a secret base
where they built and tested the last big
tank. That base was abandoned in 1943.
There's another one at Needles, California,
and Ibiss is another one. Laguna base is
south of Yuma, then there's Camp Young north
of Desert Center in California. Iron
Mountain is fenced so you can't get in there
any more," Bill said.
    "They ran us off one time," Beryl said.
"They're still using some of these areas as
test sights for new guns, and planes are
dropping bombs all over the place.
Sometimes they have a helicopter checking out
the sight before the testing begins so they
don't kill too many crazy Snowbirds. We were
out there just hunting away when this
helicopter lands and the guy tells us to get
out of there before we get our heads blown
off. We didn't waste any time," Beryl said.
    "I was going to wait a while then go

back, but Beryl was chicken," Bill said.

"I told him to take me home! He may need that kind of excitement in his life, but he doesn't need to be dragging me into it. I can get along just fine with the excitement we already have without living dangerously in a bomb testing area. Crazy old man!" Beryl added.

"When you come over to Yuma I'll show you some of the things we've picked up," Bill said. "The young guys that lived in tents on the desert must have thrown away everything they had. You can pick up dog tags, wedding rings, crucifixes, silver bars, medals, bracelets, high school rings and all kinds of silver coins. Beryl found one pin that said, 'Japan started it, we'll finish it'. I know one old man that has five gallon buckets full of coins and stuff sitting around his house. He's been hunting on some of these bases since 1941. He said it wasn't uncommon to pick up two buckets full every time he went out. Beryl and I have thousands of silver coins. Beryl keeps hers separated from mine. She's a bearcat to hunt with."

"We're total enemies when it comes to hunting coins. We're also jealous if one gets more than the other. I pick my spot and draw a square in the dirt to mark off my territory. Nobody better come anywhere near!" Beryl said.

"At Camp Ibiss and Needles it's posted that you can't excavate artifacts. We called the BLM to see if we could hunt at Needles and they told us we can pick up anything lying on the ground but you can't excavate. An artifact is anything that is 50 years old or older. Coins aren't considered to be artifacts. Most of the coins we find are close or laying right on top of the ground. Every time it rains it washes up a new batch," Bill said.

"I wonder if we're considered to be

artifacts? We're over 50," Eddie asked.

"Did we ever tell you about our trip to
Florida in Cork and Bernita's motorhome?"
Waldo asked. "We had a lot of fun. We only
had two weeks so had to make every minute
count. We traveled from 'can't see till
can't see' then we'd stop at a motel and get
a room. Margaret and Eddie and Norma and I
would sleep in the motel and the Browns would
stay in the RV in the parking lot." One
night we couldn't find a motel so stopped at
a rest area and slept a while. We all found
a place to lay down but it sure was noisy
with the trucks coming and going all night."

"Tell them about Eddie and the bridge,"
Margaret said.

Waldo continued his story, "We were
taking turns driving, and Ed was at the
wheel. We had driven all night when we came
to a bridge under construction over the
Missouri River. They detoured us around to a
rather narrow bridge. There was a whole
string of 18 wheelers coming from the other
side as we made our way onto the bridge. The
bridge had big steel abutments that stuck out
on both sides as a support to help hold it
up. We clipped every one of those protruding
arms with the rear view mirror and the
awning. It sounded like the whole side of
the motorhome was being ripped off. Margaret
covered her head, threw herself on the floor
and hollered. 'Eddie, you just bought
yourself a motorhome!' Broken mirrors were
laying all over the bridge as the trucks on
the other side were losing their mirrors
too."

"We're going over the side! We're going
over the side!" I hollered, then I covered my
eyes and prayed. It was the longest bridge I
have ever seen. I didn't think the end would
ever come. When we finally arrived safely on
the other side, we spotted a Sambos
restaurant and decided since they gave

discounts if you had a Good Sam card, it would be a good place for breakfast. Good Sam is a club especially for RV owners. We all bailed out to survey the damage and were very surprised to find the one mirror was all that was damaged. The awning was scratched a little but not beyond repair. We really felt lucky to get out of that one alive. Thank God."

"Let me tell you about the big discount we received for breakfast," Norma said. "We let Bernita take all the money for the breakfast tickets since she had the Good Sam card. When she went to the cash register and showed her card the waitress told her they didn't accept Good Sam cards anymore, but she would be glad to give her a senior citizen discount."

"I went ahead and took the discount all the while feeling a little bit guilty for doing so. You see at that time I was only 42 years old. Just because my hair had been grey since I was 25 didn't make me a senior citizen," I said, as our smart-alec group was laughing their heads off.

"From that time on we let her be in charge of paying all the bills and nobody ever questioned whether she was truly a senior citizen or whether she had dyed her hair grey just so she could get the discounts," Norma said.

"This has certainly been an interesting conversation tonight, but I think it's time we had a little music and a sing-along," Dick said.

Bob, Pat and Waldo found their instruments and started tuning up. Dee and Maxine were ready to sing and joined right in with their rendition of "Once More To Be With You Dear." Dick, Jeri, Eddie and Cork gave us a dazzling version of quartet music that would top any barbershop group I have ever heard. We named them the "Desert Dandies".

Bill and John took turns dancing with all the girls and it wasn't long until we were having our own little hoedown. There seemed to be one thing missing, and Will soon came up with the answer. He started beating on an old bucket, using it for a drum, then our band was complete.

We finished the evening with a sing along of gospel music. "The Old Rugged Cross", "Amazing Grace", and "Give Me That Old Time Religion" were ringing from North 53rd Street to Snowbird Lane and to the depths of the kangaroo rat holes. We closed by holding hands in a circle around the campfire and some of us offering a prayer for our troops and for all the innocent and hungry people who were spending the night in a far off desert where love and fellowship were nowhere to be found.

Chapter Nine

THE POW WOW

The day of the big Pow Wow dawned much too early when we were all awakened to reveille on Bill's musical horn. That by itself wouldn't have been so bad but LaVern jumped out of bed and started answering back with her horn. We could handle "Yankee Doodle Dandy" and "Home On The Range", but LaVern couldn't keep herself from playing "Boomer Sooner". Them's fightin' words for those of us from Nebraska, but no doubt she knew it would rout everyone out of bed.

The men finished their bathroom chores in record time that morning so they could be the first ones out to start discussing football or cussing the Sooners. The fact that at least half of our group of Nebraskans are transplanted "Okies" always produces a lively discussion when it comes to football.

Since the guys had their attention on football while they had their morning coffee, I decided I wanted to sneak a shower. If I abided by the rules for showers that had been spelled out to me earlier, my mate would never know that I had showered instead of finger bowled. It was heavenly, even if I was the last one ready to go that morning.

We piled into three vehicles, car-pooling so that we wouldn't have trouble finding places to park. The problem was everybody and his dog were already there ahead of us. We finally found a place about two miles from the show. The QIA (Quartzsite Improvement Association) had a modified hay wagon for people to ride from the far-out parking lots, but there were too many people looking for a ride.

"We should have walked from camp and saved about a mile," Cork said.

The weatherman was co-operating fully. I'm sure the QIA put in a special order. The clearing sky was full of jet stream trails that looked like crinkled crepe paper ribbons strung across a room. The warmth of the day felt like an ideal June afternoon on the golf course in Kimball, Nebraska. We had already shed our jackets and were looking forward to the big event. This was the first day of the Pow Wow and it was supposed to be an extra special event because of the 25th Anniversary celebration.

The QIA's first year was 1965. A group of local residents and winter visitors got together and formed a Community Group. Their first project was a Rock & Gem Show held in

February, 1967.   At that first show there
were eight displays inside and about twenty
dealers outside.   Attendance was estimated at
1,000.   Little did they know how their idea
would mushroom into a gigantic production.
The past twenty years of Pow Wows have
greatly improved over the first few.   This
year there are 500 outside dealers, 17
dealers on the inside and 60 showcases with
outstanding displays in the center of the
building.

The QIA has done more for Quartzsite than
put on the Pow Wow.   The Medical Center, the
Library, and the Fire Department were all
started by the QIA.   Television was brought
to Quartzsite by the QIA and is financed by
them.   They also keep up the cemetery and the
Hi Jolly Tomb.   Hadji Ali (Hi Jolly) was an

Arab camel driver who came to the desert in the mid-1850s. The U.S. Army had ordered the camels for a desert experiment. The experiment didn't work out and the camels were sold at auction. Hi Jolly died in 1902. His grave, marked as the centerpiece of the cemetery is a large pyramid made of the stones found in the Quartzsite area and is topped with a little copper camel. The townspeople have a special celebration they call Hi Jolly Days, being held in November 1991.

Today the QIA has over 800 members. Many Snowbirds are active, industrious members of the Association. Without their volunteer help, there wouldn't be an Association.

The QIA building is used for all kinds of activities when the Pow Wow isn't running; for a meeting room, recreation hall, and best of all a place for single and married Snowbirds to gather for fellowship and a good time. I visited with Nancy Ann Luker who was giving out information at the QIA booth. She said, "We had a permanent trailer in a court here for six years before I lost my husband. I decided to keep coming back and really enjoy the singles group that meets at the QIA building. We do lots of fun things, there are dances on Wednesday and Saturday nights, every Friday morning the club takes a trip to the desert, and Friday evening is bingo. About a year ago I met a man from Missouri. We dated for a while and then got married. Last year six couples married that had met here at the singles club."

On March 1, 1990, at the meeting of the Quartzsite Roadrunners Gem and Mineral Club, the members had a big surprise. David Taylor picked that day to have his wedding. It seems the lady he was to marry was surprised, too. When the minister arrived, the groom was escorted to the front with a shotgun stuck in his back and some of the ladies

brought   the   unsuspecting   bride   forward.
David   and   Phyllis Meyers were   married   in
front   of   200 guests, all members of the Gem
and Mineral Club.   If   you   don't think it's
Snowbird Mating Season in Quartzsite,   just
ask Mr. and Mrs. David Taylor.

Jim   Heckathorn   was   helping   at the QIA
booth, too.   He   said, "We came here first in
1979 and have been coming back   ever   since.
The weather is what draws me to this area.   I
have a rock shop in McCall, Idaho, so I spend
the winter here and buy rocks   to   take   home
and sell."

The Quartzsite   Gem & Mineral Club had a
trailer set up   as   a   booth and were passing
out   information   about membership   in   their
club and the field trips they were sponsoring
in connection with the Pow Wow.

My interest in   rocks   began to grow as I
walked   around   the   show   viewing   the   many
displays.   I   decided   I   should   support the
club   and   paid   my   membership   dues.   The
Quartzsite   Roadrunner   Gem   &   Mineral   Club
boasts   of   more   than   600   members, most of
which are Snowbirds with hometown rock club

ties. That left us out because we don't belong to a rock club at home. I did pick up information about the field trips and left hoping to talk some of our flock into going on a rock hunting trip with me.

For their 25th Anniversary the history of the QIA was written up in the Quartzsite Nugget, a free supplement to the Palo Verde Valley Times of Blythe, California. History of the Quartzsite area can be read about in a book called, "No Ordinary Place" written by Leland Feitz. It is available at the Quartzsite Library or can be bought at the Pow Wow. The local museum is being improved all the time by the Historical Society and is worth your time to visit. Cynthia Walker and Ruth Norris were working at the Library when I stopped in for information. They were anxious to answer my questions.

Walter Barrett, who came to Quartzsite about 1970 from Washington, was a "rock hound" like many of the people who come to this desert town. He decided he wanted to build something out of rocks besides the jewelry he was making. He built a house out of stone and then started building a miniature village. He also made a replica of the Tyson Wells Stage Station and an English Castle for his granddaughter. After Mr. Barrett passed away his family donated the village to the Historical Society as a memorial to their father. The village has just recently been moved to the Historical Society grounds.

There was a solid wall of people in every aisle as we approached the show grounds. It looked and sounded like a brood of baby chickens, and I felt like one squashed in the middle as we worked our way into the crowd.

At least 75% of everything in the booths must be gem or mineral related. Every year 95% of the people who show their gems reserve a spot to return the next year. Gems, gold and minerals come from as far away as Brazil, Africa and Australia. Dealers and visitors come from Canada, the USA, and Switzerland to participate in the show. In-house security guards are on duty 24 hours a day to protect the valuables.

Part of our group decided we had to venture into the QIA building to view the fabulous displays. "Come on you guys, we may find a diamond or two we can't live without," Beryl said.

"I don't know why men don't get excited about jewels and some of the finer things in life," I added. "Come on, let's go without them." The displays were spectacular.

One of the local silversmiths, Scott Watson, had a display of Crackpot Jewelry. His jewelry depicts how Indian pottery may be found out in the desert. He does intricate

cliff dwellings that have tiny fine ladders
on them. To see all the fine details, you
would have to carry a magnifying glass. He
uses sterling silver, gold and copper and
combines them into very unique pieces. There
are never two pieces alike. Besides his
showcase display inside the building, he also
had a booth on the show grounds.

T.J. Lane's jewelry, in one of the cases
inside the hall was awe-inspiring. The
delicate heart-shaped pendants are uniquely
designed with flowing textured lines to
delight the eye.

"If we could just get our husbands in
this place, wouldn't they have a ball buying
us these beautiful jewels?" I asked LaVern
and Beryl. They were soon lost in the craft
room while I continued to stare in awe at the
jewelry. I finally decided I was just
dreaming and settled for a Quartzsite Pow Wow
sweatshirt and the book, "No Ordinary Place".

We all agreed that the QIA, all of its
members and the many volunteers that it takes
to put on a show of this magnitude, deserved
a special award for their outstanding work
for such a monstrous project. It is well
organized and runs like a well-oiled machine.

I knew I wouldn't be able to leave
without buying at least one rock-related
item. I had been looking at book ends made
from cut rocks and decided that's what I
wanted. I stopped at a booth to look at some
bookends and visited with Larry and Virginia
Kribs from Bend, Oregon. He said he was
semi-retired and spends part of his time here
at Quartzsite in the winter. By trade he is
a home-builder, but represents the Desert Dog
Mines in Dry Creek, Oregon, selling
thundereggs. Everybody but me knew what a
thunderegg was. They are medium-sized red
rocks and when cut reveal quartz, opalite and
red jasper. I thought they were pretty and
invested in a pair for my office at home.

The guys were busy watching some of the
displays of working lapidary equipment.
Lapidary, as explained to me, means the
cutting, polishing, carving and engraving of
gems. "Just think," Norma said, "if they
learn how to cut and polish gems we can start
hunting rocks and they can make all of our
jewelry from now on." Waldo gave us a
disgusted look and started moving down the
next aisle.

As we were rounding a corner near the
south end of the show grounds, we came upon a
booth full of weird looking masks like witch
doctors wear in the African jungles. They
also had skeletons and skulls of people.
Unless these ugly items were made from rocks
I couldn't see where their booth was 75% gem
and mineral related. It was eerie, freakish
and ghostly, and made me feel uneasy. One

character was dressed in buckskins and furs.
They probably would have been an interesting
group to talk to, but I decided against it.
"Where do you suppose they get the skulls and
skeletons?" I asked my mate.

"They probably get them from Snowbirds
that stand around asking dumb questions and
snooping into their business," he answered.
So we quietly moved on.

Our group was all congregating by the QIA
building where the men had found a bench to
sit on. We all gathered up our treasures and
headed for the Four Corners area. The first
thing we saw there was someone selling Oregon
Cream with a sign that said, "Rub it wherever
you have a pain". I knew someone would have
a smart crack for that one and I didn't have
long to wait.

John piped up, "My wife's a pain. Will
it work on her?"

We all headed for a booth selling tee
shirts, three for $10. As we were stocking
up for the family, suddenly the air was
filled with what sounded like music from a
small organ. A man's voice penetrated the
other noises around us, gently singing and
playing old country favorites. Ron Gilson
was playing the Omnichord, a small instrument
made by Suzuki. I listened as he talked to
the people gathering around his booth. "This
instrument makes it possible for you to sound
like a pro, even if you have never played
before. It is a combination of musical
instruments in a light weight portable
machine. Omnichords are strummed like a
guitar. You can add chords, rhythms, bass
and drums to your favorite songs without
knowing one note from another. You can learn
to play in minutes."

One of my secret desires has been one day
to be able to sing and play an instrument
like a guitar, but unfortunately, God did not
bless me with that kind of talent. I always

figured it would have to be in my second
life. That conjured up visions of me
floating around on a cloud like an angel
playing a harp, or why couldn't it be an
Omnichord? If what Ron says is true, I can
buy it now and be ready to play along tonight
as our group gathers around the campfire.

My husband did his disappearing act again
when he saw me step up and take my turn at
trying to play. I took a short lesson from
Ron and was singing and playing within
minutes. He was a good salesman. A good
looking salesman too. Ron said he lives in
Northern California, runs a gold mine, plays
golf and sells Onmichords. What a
combination! What else is there in life,
except those mentioned? Well, maybe I could

come up with one more characteristic I would
want in a mate, _if_ I were in the market.
When I told him I was writing a book and the
name was to be Snowbird Mating Season, he let
me know right quick how lucky he was to have
a lovely mate who enjoys their lifestyle to
the fullest! Some days are like that. I was
going to tell him I had a mate too, but he's
never around when I need him, especially when
I'm thinking of spending money.

There were interesting people running
around everywhere you looked. Several were
handicapped and unable to do the strenuous
walking that goes with attending an event of
this magnitude. I stopped to talk to a very
pleasant grey-haired lady who was riding in a
battery operated cart because she couldn't

handle the walking.   She   had   a sign on the
front   of   her   cart   that   said   "Shirley's
Cadillac".   Shirley   and   Cliff   Stoneburner
were from the Phoenix area.   Shirley said,

"We first came   here   about   eight   years ago
pulling a 13' trailer. We parked   our little
trailer   in   the boondocker's area right nèxt
to a bunch of 40' expensive motorhome busses.
One morning I was sitting outside my trailer

in a lawn chair, still in my housecoat, when a man came along and wanted to take my picture. He was writing a story for a magazine and wanted to compare the different sizes of motorhomes, and the different kinds of people who were known as boondockers. I never did see it in print."

We passed a lady very attractively attired in a skirt and blouse, hair perfectly groomed, but struggling with crutches on the graveled walkways. She had only one leg, while the rest of us in faded jeans and decorated sweatshirts, and all of our limbs, walk along complaining of our little aches and pains. "Let's stop and buy some Oregon Cream and quit our belly aching," LaVern said.

The Four Corners area built a new restaurant called "The Showdown." They were selling all kinds of goodies, so we stopped to have a piece of pie, and I continued to watch everything I put in my mouth. The restaurant also served as a meeting place for different groups. We stopped and picked up information on a dinner show and seminar on gold mining. There is a group of gold miners called the Modern Gold Miners & Treasure Hunter's Association which has get-togethers in different areas around California and Arizona. They give seminars on metal detecting and basic gold mining. This group was also having a big music hoedown in connection with the seminar. "I think you guys ought to take the seminar on gold mining before we head out into the desert to look for our fortune," Maxine said.

"We already have an expert metal detector, Bill knows all about it, he can teach us," Jeri said.

"We'll have our own hoedown at camp tonight," Eddie added. "Bernita bought that Omnichord, it's going to turn our musical group into a first class hoedown."

Part of our group was talking about moving on the next day, so we decided to start working our way back to the pickup. We had given up on trying to keep everyone together. Actually it was impossible. We needed to rest for a while before the evening entertainment started.

If we were lucky the guys would cook supper while we lounged around. Bill and Waldo liked to cook on the grill. John liked to make fried potatoes. The rest of the men's favorite thing to do was sit around and boss. They don't want to cook but they know how it should be done. We gals could start a bridge game and leave the guys to their jobs. We wouldn't ever think of interfering with anyone willing to cook.

It looked like a little rain cloud coming up as the smell of John's potatoes drifted through the open window of the motorhome. John wasn't taking any chances on letting Maxine have anything to do with his boondocker potatoes. He took his electric skillet outside and plugged it in. The smell of onions, bacon and potatoes cooking together awakened the hunger pangs, and we decided it was time to get the tables set. We were about half through the meal when a whirlwind came through camp picking up the three inches of loose dirt and sand that was on the trail leading in and out of our camping area. We made a mad dash to cover everything to keep the sand out. The wind and sand blew for about five minutes, then calmly settled down. We finished our dinner grinding the gritty sand between our teeth, pretending everything still tasted good.

"Does this happen very often?" Margaret wanted to know.

"We've been coming to Quartzsite for many years and I've never seen anything like it," Beryl said. "Sometimes we have a day that the sand blows all day, but not like this."

We washed the dishes and cleaned up the mess the guys made trying to cook, while they started building the fire getting ready for a relaxed evening around the campfire. The fire was reaching up to tickle the heavens, and our bodies all settled into lawn chairs when another sand storm hit. We couldn't see two inches in front of our face. Lawn chairs went flying, huge raindrops fell and the fire was leaping way out of control.

I groped for the motorhome door, managed to get it part way open, while Cork was screaming for me to get in the RV. With his help I finally pulled the door open. I looked at myself in the mirror and I was black, my hair and everything else was full of sand. Our clothes were plastered and everything inside the motorhome was covered with sand. The storm lasted ten or fifteen minutes and then dissipated.

"So this is what they call a Desert Storm," I said to Cork. We had to have baths and wash our hair. Tomorrow would just have to be our day to fill up with water. When Cork looked down at the bottom of the shower, he was standing in a sandy mud hole.

"Boy, we've had dirt storms at home but I've never seen anything like this," he said. When a few of us were brave enough to venture back outside and hunt up our lawn chairs everybody started complaining.

"We're not staying here any longer," Bev said.

"We're getting out of here as soon as we make the rounds and pick up all the items we've had our eyes on for the last two weeks," Dee said.

The guys doused the fire in case another tornado came by. "We're lucky we didn't set the world on fire with the bonfire we had going, mixed with that wind it could have been deadly," John said.

The next day there were people running

around looking for coolers, lawn chairs, buckets and everything imaginable. There were also lots of people moving out, but many new Snowbirds were taking their place. The word was around town that the dirt storm was a small twister. Many of the vendors had their tarps blown down and the framework badly twisted and bent from the severe winds. Merchandise had been scattered up and down the aisles. The vendors were busy helping each other get their stands put back together. The damage was quickly repaired and it wasn't long until it was business as usual.

"Are you sure you don't want to stay a few more days?" I asked Eddie and Margaret. "There are places we haven't even been yet, and don't forget the booths we have marked to go back to a second time. We're going on a field trip out to Crystal Hill and see if we can't find our own rocks to make jewelry, and maybe hunt for gold. We might even get up our own golf tournament in the desert."

"If you're going to have a tournament we'll stay, but what do we do if one of those terrible sand storms comes up in the middle of our golf game?" Eddie wanted to know.

"We'll be sure we put something about desert storms into the rules when we make them up," I told him.

Chapter Ten

THE FAMILY BACK HOME

Making a phone call from Quartzsite during the time when the shows are running is an experience that tries the patience of even the mild-mannered Snowbird. Bill said, "Be sure you call the family before you get to Quartzsite and let them know that you'll be away from the phone for about 10 days. If you ever do find a phone, all you'll receive is a recorded message that says, 'all long distance lines are busy'."

We managed to get along for a few days without calling home before we felt like we had to be sure everything was running smoothly. We own and operate a water well drilling business. Two of our sons are employed with us, but the boss still has to call home every once in awhile just to be sure everything is going O.K. Cork isn't completely retired yet and still likes to think our sons need his advice. We told the boys our whereabouts and if there were an emergency, the police would be able to find us.

We borrowed John's car and headed for the telephone booths early in the morning so we wouldn't have to wait very long. But we had to wait and wait and wait. By the time it was our turn for the phone booth, we knew just how everything was supposed to be done. The man ahead of us kept re-dialing one time right after the other. "The trick is to be just a hair faster than the other guy," he said.

We waited an hour and a half to get into the booth and another 30 minutes trying to get a line out of town. There were four phone booths and 30 people waiting to call. When we finally reached our home office, the guys had already gone to work and the ever-present answering machine was quick to reply. The phone booths we tried to use were to the south of Tyson Wells Sell-A-Rama. Many of the people standing in the line waiting to use the phones were vendors from that area. Some of them were trying to contact their suppliers to order more merchandise. They were upset because the Snowbirds were holding up the phone lines.

We decided it would be best to find another area to call from after the crowd was tired of shopping and had gone home to rest. Later that day John and LaVern decided they would check in with their daughter and let her know they were O.K. and be sure all was well at home. They went through the same ordeal we had that morning. When they finally got an answer, it was the answering machine with this message: "Hello, this is the Strasheim summer home, som'r home and some aren't." LaVern stuck her tongue out and went, "Ppffft to you, too."

I had some things I wanted to tell our sons. I had left them with a list of chores to do when they were caught up on their work. They might as well have something to do while sitting around waiting for someone's well to freeze up.

The list had important things on it and read as follows:

1. Replace the kitchen faucet.
2. Install new light fixture in the office.
3. Poop scoop the yard.
4. Water my plants, but don't drown them.
5. Paint the kitchen ceiling.
6. Clean my garage.
7. Feed the cat and dog.
8. When scooping snow from the patio be sure you throw some on my tulip bed.
9. Most important of all, send money whenever we holler.

I also wanted to check and see how much work they had been doing, and to be sure they made out statements regularly so the money would keep coming in. What a switch, letting the kids worry about how to pay the bills and whether to send mom and dad money!

Living the life of a Snowbird might be cheap for some people, but I haven't figured that out yet. There was too much stuff here to buy. "If you come here every year, you have to learn how to limit your spending," Beryl said.

"Maybe somewhere around here they give a course on controlling spending," I said. "Then again, after we figure it out ourselves we could start a class and teach others."

Everywhere we went that day we kept an eye out for phones that weren't crowded. We headed for the east side of town and Cloud's Jamboree. There were phones by the parking lot right close to where we parked. They were busy, but no waiting line. We all made a mad dash for the phones and started a line by each one.

We finally reached our business and found that everything was going fine, and all the family were healthy. Jerry had checked on great-grandma and grandpa and all was well. With aging parents one never knows what will happen next, or when.

"Have you had time to do the jobs on my list?" I asked.

"We've been so busy we haven't had time to even look at your list. Matter of fact we don't even know where it is," Jerry answered. "Besides, if we do all that stuff what are you going to do when you get home?"

I don't know where he gets all of his smart-alecness, but he was as sharp as a freshly-broken piece of quartz that day.

Some of us are just practicing our retirement to see if we are going to be able to handle it. We still need to maintain communications with our business. Waldo is Drilling Superintendent for an oil well drilling company. He needs to check with his office every day. After we found the telephones at Cloud's, the phoning job became easier.

The police department, in Quartzsite, receives many calls every day from people looking for their friends or family. We told our family where we would be before we left home. But, when an emergency did come up, the police went to Tyson's and posted a note on the bulletin board. We didn't even know there was a bulletin board in Tyson's area. It is very important for anyone coming to

Quartzsite for the Pow Wow, or to stay for
the winter, to leave word with the family as
to which area they are in, and then to watch
the bulletin boards in that area. Trying to
find two Snowbirds in Quartzsite would be
like trying to sort out two particular
Canadian geese from a flock of 50,000. It's
next to impossible, but much easier if they
know your area.

    As long as we were at Cloud's Jamboree,
we thought we might as well look around and
see what kind of bargains we could find.
Basically, it was more of what we had been
seeing all week. We did find some items we
couldn't live without. Collars and neck
scarfs decorated with conchos, beads and lace
looked very inviting. The collars and scarfs
were made out of men's handkerchiefs, which
now come in every color imaginable.

    Ann Taylor from Chico, California, was a
vendor that I couldn't pass by.

I first noticed she was selling neck pillows, made especially for all sizes of necks. "I need one of those for the motorhome when we are traveling so I don't jerk my head off when I fall asleep," I told the girls. Before I left her booth she succeeded in selling me two neck pillows and a billfold that I didn't need. Why? She's a good salesperson and because I could see that she was crippled. A very brave and trusting lady. She didn't even ask for identification on our checks. "God only brings me honest people," she said. Her husband sells custom made screens for motor homes. He was out installing when we were there. Ann and her husband make their living going from one craft fair to the other selling their home-made products.

We had been looking for a lady from Elwood, Nebraska, who had a booth called "Aw-Shux" cornhusk dolls.

"I'm sure she was at Tyson's last year," Beryl told us.

The reason we couldn't find her was because she was here at Cloud's. Jay & Kaye Evans were selling cornhusk doll music boxes. Kaye's daughter was there helping make the dolls. They moved to Cloud's Jamboree from Tyson's after selling there for many years. I asked her why? "They kept jacking the rent up every year, we weren't making any profit, so we relocated."

Kaye told a very romantic story about how she met her mate after her first husband died. "I went to the hospital to visit my brother-in-law. Jay and I went to school together 50 years ago, and he held my hand in our class play, but I hadn't seen him for 42 years. He came over and gave me a big hug. The sparks started flying right away and I knew that I wanted Jay for my next husband."

Jay had never been married. He was a Mason, bowled a lot and enjoyed camping. He

was a retired farmer who was spending his
winters in Arizona, most of the time at Slab
City. He was too shy to meet girls. "I was
traveling then too, selling my cornhusk doll
music boxes. I was doing shows all over the
west from San Diego to Seattle. I had just
finished a show at Scottsdale and was headed
for Phoenix. I worried that Jay didn't like
me and I finally decided to go see him at
Slab City because he wasn't going to come see
me."

The exciting part of this story is they
did get married, and Jay took her to
Quartzsite for their honeymoon.   They have a
home at Johnson Lake near Elwood, Nebraska,
where they live in the summer. Kaye's eyes
sparkled like diamonds and her smile was as
wide as a grinning pumpkin as she told me
her story.   Is it Snowbird Mating Season in
Quartzsite? "Yes!" says Kaye, "We've had
eight good years and we've enjoyed that many
years in Quartzsite during Snowbird Mating
Season."

Jay had a stroke last summer, so he won't
be able to travel to all the shows this year.
Her daughter will be running the booth and
Kaye will still be helping by making the
cornhusk dolls for the music boxes. Now they
will be part of the family back home, trying
to keep up with a traveling daughter who will
be in Quartzsite trying to find a telephone
that's not busy and taking part in Snowbird
Mating Season.

Chapter Eleven

A TRIP TO CRYSTAL HILL

I talked my husband and John and LaVern into taking one of the field trips offered by the Quartzsite Roadrunner's Gem & Mineral Club. I promised them we would find all kinds of gems. All they had to do was get off their duff and do a little searching. Crystal Hill was supposed to be full of crystal. People have been digging around on the hill for years, and there is still crystal there for the taking. "If other people can find it so can we," I told them.

Bring plenty of water, your own lunch and furnish your own transportation, the flyer from the club said. We were to meet at mile marker 103, south on Highway 95. We arrived early and took our place in a line of vehicles that was already forming.

Kenneth Otterstrom was our wagonmaster. We registered with him, and he showed us samples of the quartz that we would be looking for. Mile marker 103 was across from LaPosa West, one of the $25 fee camping areas run by the BLM. Thousands of trailers and motorhomes were scattered like my grandkids' toys all over the area.

It was a still morning with a clear sky streaked with the ever present ribbons of jet streams. While waiting to leave on our excursion, one of the many trailers burst into flames. We had ringside seats to a very sad experience. The rolling black smoke

QUARTZSITE

FIREFIGHTERS ASSN.

spiraled into the air as people in surrounding RV's started running to help. We watched as neighbors close by brought people out of the trailer and dashed to get blankets and fire extinguishers. The trailer was enveloped with flames in a matter of minutes. We could hear the whine of the fire truck's sirens in the distance. There was too much traffic so it was hard for the firemen to maneuver into the area where the trailer was.

We could only guess that the cause of the fire was whatever they were using to heat the trailer. It gets cold on the desert at night and most of the time you need heat of some kind. John started telling us all the do's and don'ts of heating an RV. "Don't ever try to heat with your oven or the burners of your cookstove. We never run our furnace at night here. It gets cold, but not that cold, so we pile on a bunch of blankets and don't need to turn up the furnace until morning. Do check your RV periodically for propane leaks. It doesn't hurt to have one of the new smoke alarms that also has a gas sniffer on it. If you take the time to use a little caution, accidents like this one won't happen," he said.

"There's one pair of Snowbirds that won't have a place to roost tonight," Cork said.

It was finally time to start our trip as 32 cars pulled out into the line of traffic following the wagonmaster. We turned east and formed a drawn-out procession, watching the dust clouds roll while we rumbled along on the washboard road for about five miles.

When we arrived at our destination everybody jumped out and took off up the rocky hill on the run, wanting to be the first one to find the treasure. We were greenhorns about hunting for rocks and had no idea what to bring to dig with. We managed to come up with a hammer and two screwdrivers.

"That's O.K. I'll find the spot and point, you guys can dig, and when we find the jewels I'll carry them," I told Cork and John.

When I glanced up it looked like a bunch of ants swarming over an ant hill as everyone spread out. My mate lasted about 30 minutes. He climbed back down the hill, into the wash, and sat down in the shade of a Palo Verde tree to drink a pop. LaVern was having trouble with her leg and chose to sit in the car and read a magazine.

John, with his hammer and screwdriver, was chipping away at a rock, searching for his treasure. There was a bunch of loose rock as I slipped and almost tumbled to the bottom of the hill. I spied a man that was fully equipped and looked like he knew what he was doing. I inched my way to a sturdy looking rock, perched upon it, and watched to see if he were finding any of the illusive crystal that we were all supposed to find.

I started asking questions, and he was very willing to talk about rockhounds, and how he had become one. The man's name was Al Mumsick, he was from Pittsburg, Pennsylvania. He spent most of his life as an iron worker and had recently retired. Now, he and his wife travel around the country in search of different rocks and gems. Al said, "We came to Quartzsite for the Rock & Gem Show. We took a few days and went to Laughlin and lost some money, now we're back to rock hunting."

Al had knee pads, hiking boots, a string to hold his glasses on and long leather gloves. He had a back pack along to carry his tools and any treasures he might find. His jeans and shirt were covered with dirt as he shed his coat and was getting down to business. He kept quite busy all the while he talked, and was using a wedge he made out of an old automobile spring. "You cut off about eight inches of the spring and taper

the end so that it will fit down into the
cracks in the rock. Then all you do is
hammer it in and your rock breaks easily," he
said. Now why hadn't we thought about that?
We could have stripped the car of its springs
before we climbed the hill.

Al found several pieces of good looking
crystal and showed me what we were supposed
to be looking for. "There's a lot of the
milky quartz, but mixed with it is some
inclusions of the clear crystal," he said.
It dawned on me that this is probably where
Quartzsite got its name, from having so much
quartz in the area. Al gave me several small
pieces of crystal he chipped out, and I stuck
them in my pocket to take home as a souvenir.

"If you want to see some pretty gems,

stop at our motorhome and see the Herkimer diamonds that we found in Herkimer, New York," Al said. "We go to Tombstone, Arizona, and hunt through the tailings of the mines and find azorite and pieces of turquoise. Now we plan to travel to Cowee Valley, North Carolina, where you can find rubies, sapphires and emeralds."

Al suggested I buy a book by Frederick Pough, all about gems and minerals. I'm not sure if he was tired of answering my questions or thought I was really interested in learning more about rockhounding. I decided I better move on as I noticed someone digging a little farther around the steep edge of the hill. I was sure it wasn't anyone from our group, so maybe he knew what he was doing. I dug my fingers into the face of the rock and inched my way closer.

The person turned out to be a young man about 19 years old. He had his head and shoulders in a hole in the rock, laying on his back, chipping away, totally absorbed in his work, trying to find a large piece of crystal. The sweat was trickling down his face as the dust clung to his sticky, sweaty body like the dirt storm the night before had stuck to us. He smelled like it had been a few days since he had seen a shower. So who cares? If I never learn anything else about boondocking, I have learned that it's all right if you have B.O. I may not ever get used to it, but it's all right.

My new friend was Mike Garcia from Eugene, Oregon. Mike was a friendly young man with long, black, stringy hair, a few tufts of hair on the chin where a beard would have grown if it could, a hole in the seat of his pants, Indian beads around his neck, a sleeveless Mickey Mouse tee shirt and a huge smile. He was living in a little tent next to the parking area.

"My friends and I stopped here last night and camped, and we found a big piece of crystal," he said, "but don't tell anyone. It has ten fingers of crystal on it," he continued. "My friends had to travel on to Tucson, but after I found that big piece I wanted to stay here and look for more. I don't have the proper equipment to dig with, but this guy over here said he would give me one of his wedges." He went on to tell me how very carefully you have to dig to keep from breaking the crystal from the rock. "It's not worth as much if it's broken," he said. "If you want to see my big piece I'll take you down to my tent as soon as I finish this part I'm working on."

"I would love to see it," I told him. I

suppose this is what some people call a desert rat. My mate thinks I'm always sticking my nose into places where it doesn't belong, wait till he sees me headed to the tent with this young man, and to the motorhome with Al. But, how else can you possibly learn anything if you don't stick your nose in and ask questions? It was a lot more fun to ask questions and to see the actual prize than to sit down and read a book about it.

"I thought I was being invaded this morning when I looked up and seen that long procession of vehicles rumbling this way with a cloud of dust two miles long," Mike said, as we walked down the hill towards his tent.

"Are you going to school anywhere?" I asked him.

"No, I graduated from high school and I want to go to school and get a degree in drafting and blue printing. Right now I have to try and sell the crystal I found to help pay my way back to Oregon," he said.

As we were coming down the hill we met a man from Pasco, Washington. His name was Vaughn Montvale, and he was walking with two canes. As he tried to work his way up the hill he told us he had emphysema. "Now I wish I'd brought my wheel chair so I could ride back down," he said.

My mate saw me walking with Mike and came to meet us and see what was happening. He sauntered over to the tent with us. Mike's grin spread all over his face as he showed us his prize. I took his picture and asked him how much he thought the crystal was worth. "I hope to get $85 for it in town," he said.

I thanked him for letting me take his picture and for showing me the crystal. "Why didn't you buy the rock from him?" Cork wanted to know.

"I really didn't think I needed it, and who knows maybe it's only worth $10. I can

think of lots of other things I would rather
have, besides I've just about spent all of
our money and I don't think he would take
my credit card."

"Well, that's one good reason," he added.

We wandered back to the car and decided
to get out the lunch. We had some peanut
butter and crackers, cheese, cookies and
oranges. Just right for a snack. As we were
finishing our lunch Al came down the hill and
stopped to inquire if I wanted to see his
diamonds.

Mary Ann Mumsick, Al's wife, had spent
the morning walking up and down the wash with
her metal detector looking for gold. Al and
Mary Ann keep a log of everywhere they go and
the different kinds of rocks and gems they
find. They go back to Pittsburg and present
a program to their club. They also help give
programs twice a year to the high schools and
grade schools in their area. One of their
club members passed away and left his
collection of rocks and gems to their rock
club. "We use that in our school
presentations," Mary Ann said.

The Herkimers were dainty and sparkled
like dazzling diamonds. They come already
shaped, a very attractive stone. (For those
of you who are rockhounds, I apologize for my
feeble attempt to describe gems.)

As we checked out with the wagonmaster
and were ready to head back to camp, Kenneth
was telling a group of people that when his
wife first came out to the desert she hauled
in every rock she could find. "I learned the
hard way not to help her carry out rocks.
I'd carry one load and as soon as I returned
she'd have another bunch ready to pack out.
She thought everything was pretty and wanted
to keep them all. After a while we had to
haul a pickup load back out to the desert."

We said good-bye to our group, thinking
we were ready to leave, but LaVern had sat

all morning with the car door open and the radio on, running down the battery. Our wagonmaster just happened to have a set of jumper cables with him. "We always come prepared," he said. "This isn't the first time it's happened."

The engine kicked right off and we started out of the parking area, but I had a feeling that I should do something for Mike. Call it my motherly instinct or whatever you want, but Mike was out here in this hot sun without food or water. "Do you care if I leave the rest of our lunch by the tent for Mike?" I asked. Nobody objected so I unloaded cheese and crackers, oranges, cookies and a half gallon of water. He had a couple of warm beers sitting in the tent getting warmer. "I'd die if I didn't have anything to drink but hot beer," I said. This young man was some mother's son. I can only hope that if one of my sons was far from home and needed some mothering, somebody would leave him oranges, cookies and water.

We arrived back at camp in time for daily show and tell. Waldo found two bargains that day. He bought six sturdy lawn chairs at one of the booths selling RV supplies. "The guy gave me a bargain on six of them, I only had to pay $12 each." Everybody was interested in the chairs and Waldo started selling them. "I'll go back tomorrow and buy more," he said.

"That really was a bargain" Cork told him. "We paid $25 for those same chairs a year ago."

"What will you give me for these rakes?" Waldo started auctioning them off. "Everybody should have one of these fold up rakes to keep their campsite clean," he said. He sold all the rakes for $6 apiece. "It'll give me something to look for tomorrow, who knows I may be able to get them cheaper."

Beryl came out of her RV and announced

that she wanted to walk back to the Tyson area to pick up a quilt frame she'd seen earlier. Three of us jumped up to go along.

"There's probably some things we missed," Margaret said.

We sauntered slowly towards Prospector's Panorama Show, across the street south of Tyson's. This was one area we hadn't had time to investigate. I don't know how Beryl found it while the rest of us passed it up.

Beryl bought a quilt frame from Bennie and Bennaz Hawkins from Hastings, Oklahoma. He was a retired Navy man and spends his spare time making quilt frames, lounge chairs and rockers. She creates all kinds of crafts and they spend a couple of months in the warm country selling their wares. Their names fascinated me. She said, "We named our daughters Benee, Benondre, Betina and Debbie. If we'd had a boy I was going to name him Brix.

Beryl asked if they would be back next year in case some of the rest of us wanted to buy a quilt frame. Bennaz told us that Bennie has cancer and it doesn't look good for him, so she said it all depends on how he gets along whether they will be back another year. The Hawkins were very friendly people, and our hearts reached out to them as she told us her story when he wasn't listening.

We started back across highway 95 towards camp, when we noticed a truck of Washington apples. We stopped to buy a sack apiece, we needed something nutritious to snack on. We also spied a barbecue stand that was emitting an enticing aroma. "Why don't we buy some chicken and ribs and put it with our potato salad and beans for supper?" Norma asked.

That's the best idea I've heard all day," Margaret answered. "But, first, let's see if the guys want to take in the show at the big tent. It's supposed to be an RV, Sports & Recreation Show. Maybe they'll buy us a new

RV if we find one we like."

We all piled in the pickup and took off the back way on the access road around the south side of town. Finding a parking place anywhere near the tent would be quite a chore. Two lines of people were stretched out for 200 yards waiting to get in the door. "I'm not going to stand in line just to get in there to spend money," Eddie said.

"The line is for the Laughlin Casinos. If you stand in line you get to pull the one armed bandit and win a prize. It's usually a used deck of cards or a hat with their advertisement on it. Sometimes they give you a coupon book with all kinds of gimmicks to lure you to Laughlin so you can have a big time spending your money," Bill said.

We walked on around the lines and entered the tent to see what else was going on. All kinds of salesmen were selling everything imaginable, from RV Resorts, piggy-back trips to Mexico, RV repairs and parts, travel steam irons, sandwich makers, new plastic dishes guaranteed not ever to break, pots and pans that never stick, several vegetable choppers, and inserts for your shoes, guaranteed to keep you feet from getting tired no matter how many shows you walk through in one day.

"We've already seen most of this stuff before so it shouldn't take too long to run through here," Norma said.

I thought we had already fallen for all the food choppers on the market, but we got suckered in on another one. The salesman made carrot sticks with one stroke of his hand and chopped up a fourth of a cabbage with two strokes. Sure enough most of us bought another one.

"I need some pots and pans for the motorhome," Norma said. "And these look like a deal to beat all deals." They were. At least three of us walked out of there with new sets of pots and pans. I didn't even need them, but they sure clean up slick because they have this new kind of Teflon inside and out and it never scratches or peels off. It's a good thing they accepted credit cards.

"I can't believe you girls fall for everything, no wonder there are so many people here selling junk. They know there are thousands of suckers just like you, looking for a bargain," Waldo said.

"We could set up a booth selling fish worms in here and make a mint. The women would all buy some because we marked them down! It wouldn't matter if the worms are dead or even that there isn't any place to go fishing here," Dick said.

"If we bought fish worms, we'd find the Colorado River. It's around here somewhere," Beverly told him.

The men all wandered outside to look through the many RV's for sale in the lot by the tent. Gene Rucker was singing and playing his guitar in the outside theater. It was a good place to sit down and rest for a short spell.

When we walked over and started looking through the $200,000 RV busses, the guys decided it was time for us to pick up our chicken and ribs and go home for the evening.

"It's been a long day, we worked hard this morning rockhounding," Cork said.

The conversation around the campfire that night turned to other forms of entertainment besides rockhounding and wandering around the shows. The guys were getting tired of flea markets and started reminding us of the golf tournament we had promised.

"We're going to blow this place tomorrow," Maxine said. "We've gathered up all the bargains we can stand. If we buy one more thing I'll be walking home. Besides, I still have to work for a living, and my vacation time is gone."

Chapter Twelve

YUMA & NECESSARY CHORES

Friday morning was a letdown after the excitement we were used to. We were planning on traveling into Yuma to buy groceries, do laundry, clean out the motorhome and most of all, find a place to park so we could have a good shower and maybe even a hot tub and swimming pool. Since we were just "practicing" our retirement, we wanted to try out a few other adventures besides boondocking.

Everyone was standing around inside our circle of nests getting ready to say good-bye to some of our flock who were preparing to leave. In every group of Snowbirds there is at least one male bird who thinks he is God's gift to women. Our group was no exception.

All of a sudden a motorhome door flew open and our rooster started crowing for all the world to hear and see. His arms were thrown open, his chest thrust out and his words were sincere. "Here I am girls, come and get me." Then strutting like a cocky rooster, he made his way out to join the flock, as all the chicks in our group took four steps backwards. This is the same guy that stopped at the hat tables by the big tent the day before and bought three hats for $5, all of them with the saying, "Not everyone can be perfect, but somebody has to do it." Our rooster is known as Eddie. I dedicate this chapter to him.

Now that Eddie was ready to go, we said our good-bye's to Will and Dee, rice farmers from Northern California, and Jeri and Maxine. Jeri was a trucker and Maxine was the purchasing agent for a cannery, they had to go back to work. Bob and Pat were from Oregon, Bob was retired from the Navy. This was their first try at boondocking and they liked it. They were going to move to the west side of town behind the Main Event, get out their motorbikes and scout around to see what else they could find. "We may even find a gold mine in these hills," Bob said.

"We're going to find the Colorado River and check it out too," Pat said, as she pointed to the top of their motorhome where they carried a small motorboat. "When you get tired of Yuma come on back, we'll have a fishing tournament."

We were all getting ready to move out when two guys from a group that had moved in the night before, came over and started helping themselves to our wood pile. They were the L.A. Scramblers, members of the Holiday Ramblers RV Association. Don King was the wagonmaster, and Gordon King was the president of the club. "We have a camp-out on the weekends almost every month, we always enjoy coming to Quartzsite for the Gem & Mineral Show. We sure would like to have your wood if you're done with it," he said.

"You can have all you can carry," Bill told them, "Just don't let anyone take our spot, we may be back."

That was almost like telling our Cocker Spaniel not to get food on her ears. It's something you can't control. Some people rope off their section of the desert and leave an occupied sign or a lawn chair to reserve their spot. We didn't have any idea if we would be back, so there wasn't any way we could save our home in the desert. If we came back, we'd have to find a new half acre and claim it as our home away from home.

Finally we pulled our RV's out onto Highway 95 forming a procession. "Turn your CB to channel 12, there's too many trucks and other vehicles using 19, we don't want to step all over them. The truckers around here get a little perturbed at Snowbirds with their slow driving," Wild Bill said.

"We better put John in the rocking chair then," Waldo came back. (That's CB talk for the middle.)

"We need to spread out and make room for others driving faster to get around us," Bill said. He had been a trucker for many years and knew how irritated truckers can get at slow drivers. Highway 95 was two lane into Yuma so we were learning how to be courteous. "If we get a long string of people behind us, it won't hurt to pull over and let them by," Bill continued.

I rode with Beryl in the pickup to keep her company, leaving my mate to visit on the

CB with the other guys. Beryl was telling me about all the sights to see as we passed by the Kofa Mountains off to the east. "Miners called the Kofa's the shithouse mountains because they look like little outhouses. The Kofa Wildlife refuge has a small herd of burros. The BLM flew in several years ago and airlifted a bunch of them out because there were too many. The burros are in the mountains because prospectors abandoned them. A herd of wild horses used to roam the mountains too, but there are just a few of them left. Someday when you have more time, we can spend a day in the mountains and you will be surprised at the beauty and the color as you draw closer. The shades of nature in the mountains are purple, turquoise, lavender and blue. Sunset is always a spectacular show."

Beryl continued telling her story as I took notes and tried to visualize all the places she was talking about. "Another place you will want to visit sometime when you're not in a hurry is one or more of the areas that have petroglyphics. We have been to Picture Rock and Dripping Springs. That's where the early American families lived and they drew pictures on rock to leave messages for one another and to keep records. You can also see indentations in the rocks where the families ground corn and beans for meal. These are called mortar and pestil holes. We've seen several fire rings that were made hundreds of years ago. There is a program called the Arizona Site Stewards. Boma Johnson is the BLM Region I Archaeologist and is in charge of the program. These people are trained to spot Snowbirds and other tourists and local people who are chipping away at these artifacts, trying to take a piece of the Arizona desert home with them."

"It's against the law to excavate an archaeological site. Removing specimens from

a site is a class 1 misdemeanor. You can get
six months in jail and a $1,000 fine.
Damaging or defacing the petroglyphs or
pictographs is also against the law. Some
people will break off a big chunk of rock and
then find that it's too big to haul off.
Anyway, we can put this on our list to visit
when you come back next year."

We came to a road that led to Palm
Canyon. "It's a mystery as to how the palm
trees got started down in the canyon.
Mountain climbers like to crawl around trying
to reach the caves, but it's posted, warning
people not to climb there. Some have been
killed trying it anyway," Beryl said.

The different kinds of cactus were
fascinating to me. The Saguaro, the towering
cactus with gangly looking arms, was covered
with holes. "Has someone been out here
shooting holes in all those beautiful
cactus?" I asked.

"They aren't holes, they're bird's nests.
The desert woodpecker makes a hole for his
nest, then it heals itself, but he never
comes back to the same hole again. So the
cactus wren or the elf owl builds his nest in
the holes. The Saguaro can grow to 50' and
live as long as 200 years. There is one huge
Saguaro West of Quartzsite on Dome Rock Road.
We'll have to drive out and look at it next
time we're in Quartzsite. Sometimes people,
and Snowbirds try to dig the cactus and move
them into town, or take one home with them.
It's against the law to dig up any of the
plants on the desert. One guy was killed
when a Saguaro fell on him while he was
trying to dig it up. The BLM doesn't even
want you to take the dead part of the chola
cactus, which is called a jumping cactus,"
Beryl explained. "The cactus are protected
by state and federal law."

As we drove farther on I noticed we were
coming into the farm country. It seemed so

funny to see plant life after the barren desert we had been living in the last few days.

"The ground is very fertile here. As long as they can get water to the crops the sandy soil will grow anything," Beryl said. It was harvest time for cauliflower, broccoli, lettuce and asparagus. It seemed so different from Nebraska where we grow wheat, corn, alfalfa, beans and beef. No wonder we all like beans, it's one of our own commodities.

When we reached the edge of Yuma, we all pulled off into an empty lot and went in search of a place to park. We chose the Suni' Sands Mobile Home Park by the fairgrounds. It was also close to the Airbase, which wasn't too smart an idea. "It'll be O.K. Most of the planes are in Saudi Arabia," Bill told us. The campground only had three spots left so Waldo and Norma and Ed and Margaret started looking elsewhere. We were going to do all of our chores and meet at Beryl and Bill's by 10 a.m. the next day. Beryl was going to see if she could find us a place to play golf.

Our #1 priority was a refreshing shower. We had a race to see who could get there first. I'm sure the management was wondering why they ran out of hot water so early in the day. We stood under the shower and let the water run and run. It took a long time to get all the sand washed out of the hair and off the body. There are people who live out in the desert all winter, but I don't know how they survive without a good shower once in a while. If you don't mind moving your RV to fill with water every couple of days, I guess you could handle it. My mate had some words of wisdom, "You're a pansy. If you were a true outdoor person and learned what camping was actually supposed to be, you might like it."

    We will either get better at preserving
water or decide boondocking isn't for us as
we continue to practice our retirement. "Did
you get us hooked up to water so I can at
least run water to clean up this dirty
motorhome?" I asked my mate.
    "Yes, dear, everything is hooked up, let
it run."
    The saying, "The early bird catches the
worm", doesn't work with Snowbirds. Having
figured out that Snowbirds don't do anything
before 9 a.m. I decided that I could rise
early in the morning and go to the wash house
with my laundry and have it all done before
anyone else was up and around. Every stitch
of clothing we had with us was dirty. All
that walking and shopping in Quartzsite was
dirty business.
    Norma said, "You have to learn to recycle
your clothes. You wear a pair of jeans once,
then hang them up to air out, two or three
days later you wear them again and nobody
will know they aren't clean. We have more
important things to do when we're on vacation
than spending time in the laundromat."
    "That may work in some places , but it
won't work on the desert. I think there's a
limit to what you can recycle and my clothes
have reached their limit," I told her.
    I crawled out of bed early the next
morning and headed for the laundromat. There
were three wash houses in the mobile home
park and we were just across from one.
Beryl came by the night before and told us we
had a 10 a.m. tee time at the municipal golf
course, so I would have plenty of time to do
my laundry.
    No one was there when I arrived so I
started sorting my clothes. There was only
four washers so I was sorting carefully
because I knew I would have four full loads.
I had my clothes spread all over the floor in
front of all four washers when a lady walked

in.

"Which washers are you going to use?" she asked.

"I need all four," I answered.

"Don't you think I should have two?"

"There's another wash house over on the other side of the court, why don't you go there?"

"We don't do things that way here, we only use two washers apiece."

"I need all four washers! I don't have time to spend the whole day washing!" I repeated as I started shoving my clothes into the two washers closest to where she was standing.

"Well, I'll just take these other two then," she said as she ran around me and started stuffing her clothes in the other two washers.

At this point I gave up and let her have the two washers. I re-sorted my clothes, and took half back to the motorhome, fuming all the way. I had never been in a laundromat where you didn't just wait your turn when all the washers were busy. Of course, they only took two washers apiece here, that's all she needed. I couldn't believe how I let this woman bully me out of those washers. I should have just thrown my dirty underwear right in her washer, or better yet thrown her out the door. I never have liked laundromats! Now I know why. She had her husband along, where was mine when I needed him? He could have thrown them both out.

It wasn't in my nature to fight with this woman, but I couldn't forget her either. I was having some really bad feelings towards this early rising Snowbird. When I went back to move the clothes to the dryer she was talking to her husband about their plans for the day. "Did you check with the Jones's to see what time we're going to Mexico?" she asked him.

"I went by and knocked lightly, but they never answered. They could be sleeping in. There was a sign on the door that said, "If this trailer is rockin don't be knockin". It's Snowbird Mating Season you know, I didn't want to interrupt anything."

So, she had plans for the day, too, and that's why she was up early. Even while we were playing golf that day I still couldn't forget her. Why was this bothering me so much? I could get up early again the next day and do the rest of the laundry, it's no big deal! I want to attend church tomorrow, too. I had promised Bill Watkins, pastor of the Presbyterian Church in Yuma that I would visit his church the next time I was in town. I can go to bed with the chickens, or the early-to-retire Snowbirds, or maybe I'll just recycle my clothes like Norma suggested. They were all wrinkled from being hauled around in the dirty clothes basket. No! I would just have to rise early again on Sunday.

It's no wonder I was having a bad game of golf. I couldn't keep my mind on what I was doing. I had finished putting out on hole #10 when it dawned on me that I needed to forgive this lady and be forgiven myself. Looking heavenward I said a silent prayer, "Dear God forgive me for being so selfish, I may never see this woman again, but I want to forget this incident so I'm turning her over to you. I don't wish anything bad for her only that you move into her life and try to change her the way you have been trying to change me. Maybe one day we will both see how trivial this experience has been. Thanks Lord for hanging in there with me. Amen."

We enjoyed the golf game and finished on hole 19 with a cool drink. "Let's go to Tom Tate's Buffet for dinner this evening," Bill suggested. "Tomorrow we'll invite Charlie Taylor over to fix up a big Arizona style

barbecue. Come on by the house, we'll decide
what we're going to do for the rest of the
week."

"We're going to try on bathing suits
first," Norma said. "I didn't bring mine and
we have a snazzy pool and hot tub at our
place we're going to try tonight."

"Here's our chance to check out our
figure to see if we need to lose weight.
Trying on bathing suits is always an exciting
experience," Beverly said.

"It might be exciting for you, but I have
other ideas of what excitement is. Going to
a buffet for dinner is what I call exciting!"
LaVern added.

We girls all piled into one car and
started making the rounds of the department
stores in the area looking for bathing suits.
I picked up a magazine that had an article
that read: "What Suits You?   Choose a
swimsuit that flatters your figure and hides
your flaws," What a coincidence that I
should find this on a day when we are trying
on swimsuits. "Let's see, it says here that
if you have a small bosom you should wear a
strapless suit, preferably with a flowered
top drawn together in the middle with a
knot." I thought I could read this to the
girls while we were driving between stores.

"Here's one for a long, thin body, but we
don't have to worry about that one since we
don't have anybody to fit that description.
But wait, here we are, one for belly bulge or
all-over bigness. This one guarantees that
the bottom won't ride up or the fanny fall
out. It also has a tummy control panel to
disguise tummy bulge and flatten the waist,
also big bold stripes to draw attention away
from the bulge. What more could we ask for?
I think I've found the suit I'm going to look
for," I told them.

Six stores and two hours later we were on
our way home with none of us finding the

perfect bathing suit for our figures. Norma
did buy one, but it wasn't the one described
in the magazine that was supposed to cover
her flaws. The rest of us had a bathing suit
along, but we all had to face the fact that
they didn't make a suit that would cover all
our flaws. I suppose we could wear our long
sleeved, flannel, floor length nightgowns.

"That's depressing, whose idea was this
anyway? Let's go home and pick up the guys
and go to dinner. Food always makes me feel
better," Margaret said.

We had to stand in line for almost an
hour to get inside of Tom Tate's Buffet. We
were just beginning to learn that you don't
do anything in Yuma unless you stand in line,
even the laundry. The food was well worth it
though. I've never seen so much food, and I
probably have never eaten so much either.
Stuffed again.

"You know we've been hanging around
together for over a week and haven't played
cards once. Why don't we see if we can't
beat the guys at a game of Hand and Foot?"
LaVern suggested.

Hand and Foot is a game we altered to fit
our situation. It is kind of like the swim
suits; if you don't find the right one, make
your own rules and stretch it to fit. The
women always play against the men. We
adopted this game several years ago when we
were all still spending the winters in
Nebraska. We would get together every two
weeks to let the men take us out for dinner,
then we would play Hand and Foot. At first
the rules were, the losers of the game all
put $1 in the kitty. That worked fine until
the women started losing every time.

"What are we planning to do with all this
money we're gathering up by losing every time
we play?" I asked the girls.

"Don't you remember the night we started
this game and set up the rules?" Norma asked.

"We agreed to save it and one day build our own retirement center. That way we can all be together when we get too old to travel around the country."

"If that's true, then we're going to have to change the rules, or we won't have nearly enough money. Since it's all our money going into the pot I know the guys aren't going to enjoy the center because they didn't contribute to it," I said. "Remember Kaye Evans, the gal with the cornhusk dolls from Nebraska. She gave me this set of rules that can be used any time men and women are competing against each other. I think we should use them," I said.

"We're not agreeing to anything unless we see it in writing first," Waldo said.

"O.K. here they are, I'll read them."

1. The female always makes the rules.
2. No male can possibly know all the rules.
3 If the female suspects the male knows all the rules, she must change them.
4. The female is never wrong.
5. If the female is wrong, it's because the guys didn't understand the rules.
6. The female can change her mind at any point in time.
7. The male must have consent to change his mind.
8. The female has every right to be upset or angry at any time.
9. The male must remain calm at all times unless the female wants him to be upset.
10. If the female is having hot flashes the rules are subject to change without notice.

"Those are the preliminary rules, now to get down to the ground work," Margaret said. "We need to add: If the women lose, the men put in $50"

"That's a very good rule, we should have

thought of that three years ago," LaVern
said.

"Now, about this resthome business, we
need to clarify what the qualifications are
for entering. I can't remember, did you say
resthome or retirement home? It's plain to
see that we won't all be ready for the home
at the same time. I figure I'll be ready
first and I really feel like we should be
thinking about starting construction. I'm
sure I already have Alzheimer's Disease and
it will only be a matter of time until Cork
will be ready to put me away," I said.

"That's why we're in Arizona," Eddie
said. "We're picking out the ideal place to
start building our retirement center. We're
not building a resthome, we've got years
before we'll be ready for resting. We have
to make use of all the good years we have
left, then we'll think about resting.
Tomorrow we'll look around here in Yuma, then
I think we should go over to Lake Havasu and
Laughlin. We can finish up our search in the
Phoenix, Mesa area. We need to decide if we
want to buy a condominium that's all ready
built, or buy a choice piece of real estate
and start our own retirement area."

"We have a lot of decisions to make.
Maybe we want to have our own RV park. We
can decide who we want to let in. Wherever
we decide to settle for winter headquarters
has to have a golf course and access to the
Colorado River, so we can play," Cork said.

"We don't have time to waste. I've heard
of people sitting around for years talking
about their retirement, then their health
gives out and they don't ever get to enjoy
it. The first thing we have to do is get
this card game under way or we'll never be
able to afford anything," John said.

"Let's play cards before the rules get
any more complicated," Waldo added.

Chapter Thirteen

WINTER VISITORS IN YUMA

In 1990 Yuma estimated their population grew by 50,000 people at the peak of Snowbird Mating Season. In 1991 that number increased by 6%. Life in Yuma takes on a slow pace, especially the traffic. Patience is the name of the game for people who live here year round. Calls for an ambulance are definitely up as it seems like all the retired people in the world show up in Yuma, bringing with them all of their medical problems. Most Yumans love the Snowbirds because they send the economy spiraling. They can put up with the inconveniences because their pocketbooks get fatter. There are a few soreheads that wave their fists and show their tempers when the traffic doesn't move as fast as they think it should, but the Snowbirds have learned to tolerate them. Snowbirds need to learn that they aren't out in the country taking a leisurely drive and they do need to pay attention to the rules of driving.

What is it that draws Snowbirds to Yuma besides the warm weather? We set out early Monday morning to find out. We were almost like the airborne geese who excite us with their beauty and leave us wondering at the mystery of their movement. They don't know what lies ahead of them when they start their migration south for the winter. They are homeless until they find their rest in a warm haven. We were looking for a place of warmth

with enough activity to keep everybody happy
and busy. We knew what we wanted, we just
weren't sure yet where we wanted it.

We decided to start at the Yuma Adult
Center and the Yuma Civic Center. At the
Civic Center that morning, Snowbirds were
doing all kinds of crafts including wood
carving, leather tooling, beadery, knitting,
crocheting, bargello, punch embroidery, silk
flowers, bread dough, macrame chairs, and
table games. You could also get your blood
pressure checked, which we decided we all
better do just to be on the safe side for the
rest of our trip. We didn't want anybody
messing up our hunt for a retirement area by
having a stroke or heart attack.

We looked over the schedule for the rest
of the week, and it sounded like we wouldn't
have any trouble finding something for
everybody. There were silversmithing,
beginners Spanish, beginner's and
intermediate ballroom dancing and beginner's
square dance lessons. They had jam sessions,
bridge clubs, ceramics, lapidary, pool tables
and more. The Adult Center acts as a
clearing house for all the different
activities going on around town. At Marcus
Pool there are special times for senior
swimming, with lessons if you need them.

If that isn't enough to keep you busy,
there is dog racing at Yuma Greyhound Park,
and bingo at the Cocopah Bingo Hall. The
Greyhound Park is used on the weekends for
one of the biggest flea markets in the area.
You can play softball at Joe Henry Athletic
Field, all you need is your own glove and a
dollar. At the Parks and Recreation Office
you can sign up for the Senior Olympics.
Entry fee is a dollar per event. Events
include scrabble, pinochle, dart throwing,
table tennis, horseshoe, cribbage, badminton,
pool shoot, basketball shoot, bowling and
wahshoes.

"I hate to sound dumb, but I've never heard of wahshoes or bargello," I said, "but why don't we sign up for the Senior Olympics. We can golf, bowl, play softball and horseshoes. We'll sign the guys up for wahshoes and bargello, I'm sure they'll know all about it."

"You're forgetting one very important thing," Beryl told me. "You're not going to be here long enough to do everything."

"I can hardly wait to take dance lessons, I know Waldo will be as excited as I am to take ballroom dancing," Norma said. "Different trailer parks around town have dancing going on almost every night. The Gemstones play for ballroom dancing from 7:30 to 10:30 at the Golden Roadrunner Hall. The Sorta Forty Band plays big band sounds in the ballroom of the Country Roads RV Park and the list goes on of the many places that sponsor music for square dancing and ballroom dancing. The Country Roads is where we are parked. I wish we could stay long enough to take part in everything there is to do. Boy, next year we're going to be ready for this retirement business. It's sounding better all the time."

"I want to learn how to do the Country Swing and I think it would be neat to learn how to clog. You could sure lose weight clogging so I'm going to sign Cork and me up for lessons if we find a place that has them," I said.

The Arizona Western College has a Performing Arts Series with a special break on ticket prices for senior citizens. They feature Cajun music, dinner theater and country music. There's also the Yuma theater with a full schedule of entertainment.

"Boy, if we don't find something in this town to keep us busy, it's our own fault. The biggest problem will be deciding what to do first," Waldo said. "And look, here's more. There are museums, and a railroad that takes you along the winding banks of the Colorado River by the Mexico border. The train takes you to a site where you can see into four states."

"I wish we hadn't missed the big Silver Spur Rodeo," Margaret said. "Look, here they're having a big celebration called Yuma Crossing Day. Yuma was one of the few places on the Colorado River where the water was shallow enough to cross, and everyone taking the southern route to California had to cross here. The gold seekers heading for California had to ford the river on their way to Sutter's Mill. Anyway the Crossing Day is to celebrate some of Yuma's history."

"I want to go to the Yuma Territorial Prison. It's a museum now, but I can remember in the old western movies all the train robbers and the worst of the bad guys were taken to Yuma to the prison," Cork said.

"We have to go to Mexico to stock up on all the bargains over there. You guys haven't seen anything until you go into Mexico and see all the pretty Senoritas," Bill said. "They sell everything there. If you need a spare set of false teeth, they can fix you up in one day. Lots of senior citizens buy their eye glasses there too. They can bring their prescription from home and have their glasses made while they wait. Some of the people stock up on a year's supply of medicine because it's so cheap and senior citizens use medicine by the quart."

"Now that we know all there is to do here how are we going to decide what to do in the two short days we have left?" John wanted to know.

"I think we should spend some time pricing real estate and checking out the mobile home parks to get an idea of whether we want to build our own place or buy into something that's already finished," Eddie

said.   "Now that we know there is plenty here
to keep us busy, let's get started doing some
of it."

We also found out that you could take all
kinds of tours from Yuma. They had tours to
Disneyland, the San Diego Zoo, Hollywood,
Laughlin, Nevada, different places in Mexico
and many, many more.

We all decided we wanted to go to Mexico
and   spend some time bartering with the
merchants   and   maybe   even pick up some
vanilla, Mexican cookies and souvenirs for
our families back home.   We knew Charlie
Taylor who lived on the fairgrounds was busy
cooking a batch of his beef barbecue and
beans so we didn't have to worry about
dinner. But, we did have our minds on lunch
as we walked across the border into San Luis.

Curio shops lined the streets on both
sides as the merchants offered ironwood
carvings, blankets, leather goods, onyx
figures, rugs, tablecloths, pinatas and
sombreros. Dirty little children were called
into service to sell the merchants' wares,
shine shoes or just beg for a nickel, a dime,
or candy.

We found an outdoor patio restaurant and
ordered some enchiladas and tacos. The smoke
started spiraling upward from our nose and
ears as the warmth of the hot sauce settled
in around the ribs and joints. There were
some ganders in our group who raised clear up
off their chair and danced a jig.

"Boy, that stuff ought to clean the
calcium deposits out of my arthritic joints,"
Cork said. "Let's order a beer to put the
fire out."

We spent the day wandering from one
merchant to another, buying trinkets to take
home for souvenirs. We bought some all-
leather carry bags for our sons, and a
smaller version for each one of our young
grandsons to use when they travel. LaVern
and Beryl bought some huge baskets to keep
their crocheting in. We even bought crochet
thread so Beryl could make all of us some
dishcloths. Everyone had their prescriptions
from home and ordered a year's supply of
arthritis medicine and high blood pressure
pills. Sometimes when you go back through
the inspection station, the officer will ask
for your prescriptions. Then we stopped by
the grocery store and stocked up on Mexican
cookies and real vanilla.

We started looking for our mates who
disappeared when it looked like we might be
going to buy something they would have to
carry. "How could those guys abandon us in a
place like this?" Beverly wanted to know.
"Haven't they heard the stories going around
about what happens to women when they wander

away from their mates?"

"We have to be very careful not to wander too far away from the main part of town," Beryl said. "The Mexican Police are always picking up women and giving them a ticket for prostitution. They like to pick up the gringos and give them a ticket, if they don't have a valid reason they'll just make one up. That's why we don't drive the car down here. The police have been known to impound your car and throw the driver into jail for months on a simple little charge. Many groups of Snowbirds like to drive down onto the coast around Port A Penasco and buy shrimp right off the shrimp boats. We tried it once. We found out they really have delicious Mexican food. We filled the freezer in the motorhome full of shrimp, stayed all night in a mobile home park, and came back the next day. Since then we have heard some weird details about a couple who traveled down into Mexico and have never been heard from since. That was enough to scare us out of going any more."

"Well, I think it would be funny if those guys had to come bail us out of jail because we were picked up for prostitution. It'd almost be worth it to get picked up just to see their face when they found out why we were in jail," I said. "Oh shoot, here they come and we haven't even been picked up yet. What a disappointment. Let's see if they're ready to walk back across the border."

Charlie Taylor has worked many years cooking pit barbecue for the many events scheduled at the fairgrounds in Yuma. The 4-H kids were having a fundraiser that night featuring Charlie's barbecued beef. We decided there wouldn't be any better place to have dinner. He didn't disappoint us; it was delicious.

"I think we should invite Charlie and Cathey to settle in our commune when we decide where we want it to be. We're going to need a good cook," Eddie said.

"I'll certainly vote for that. I know I'm not gonna do much cookin'," Norma said, "but he may be tired of cookin' too, then what'll we do?"

"No problem, we'll just go stand in line at the many wonderful places to eat in this town," LaVern said. "What else do we have to do?"

We stopped by the post office to buy stamps and stood in line for 45 minutes. Then we went to the grocery store to pick up milk for breakfast and stood in line another 35 minutes to check out. By that time we were totally exhausted from working so hard all day and retired to Beryl and Bill's house where we all enjoyed a refreshing swim in their pool. Then we started another game of cards.

"We're going to have to play a lot of cards in the next year to be able to afford our retirement center," Eddie said.

Cork and I were invited over to the Roger Cederburgs later in the evening to see how Nebraskans live down south without a nest of their own. Roger and Ella Mae come to Yuma each fall around the end of October. They rent a condominium year round, but only live here about six months. It's cheaper to keep it rented all year with their own furniture then it is to rent a furnished apartment for six months. A lot of people don't want to be confined to a small area such as a motorhome or trailer. If you even mention having to conserve water, or not take a bath every day, they turn up their noses for sure. This type of Snowbird would never make it as a boondocker, so there are many apartments and condos in Yuma. These Snowbirds are the ones that take advantage of the activities at the Civic Center and the Adult Center.

Roger likes to play golf and plays all the courses except the Country Club. He also does volunteer work through the Lutheran Church in Yuma. The Protestant churches sponsor a project called Proyecto San Pablo. It is an outreach ministry for the Mexican people. One of their programs is teaching English classes to those applying for amnesty. Sixty Mexican babies a year are found on the desert around Yuma. The Mexicans leave them there knowing they will be well taken care of. The babies are taken to the detention center at El Centro where they are reunited with their families. Roger worked in the office setting up the books for the project.

Roger and Ella Mae volunteer in the church office and visit shut-ins delivering tapes of sermons. Many Snowbirds volunteer in any way they can to help the needy people around Yuma, all the while they are enjoying being useful in a climate that helps them keep active and healthy.

Roger told us about the Small Business Development Center at Arizona Western College. They have a plan called WAVE, Winter Visitor Expertise. They link the winter visitors who possess business experience with loyal businesses to provide a qualified counseling service at no charge to participating businesses. "If they knew you were a water well driller they would link you with a driller in this area that could use your years of experience and expertise," Roger told Cork. "A lot of retired businessmen are glad to help in any way they can, just to have something to do."

"I think they need some help with their water wells. They sure have yucky water, I can't stand to drink it," I said. "I suppose it comes from the Colorado River instead of from wells. Everytime I think of what all goes into that river, I know I don't want to drink it. We sure are lucky in Nebraska having good fresh well water. I brought several gallons of good drinking water with me, but I'm just about out. I notice they have machines that sell water by the gallon. The water at Beryl's house would corrode your insides if you drank it all the time," I added.

The next day we gathered everybody together and set out to investigate the trailer parks. We drove out west of town to a park owned by the Cocopah Indians and found they have a golf course connected with the park. The first thing we had to do was try out the golf course. We thought it was a rather short course and there wasn't any reason why we couldn't walk it. After all, we were in this country so we could get some fresh air and exercise, but at least six of us were out of shape and wished we had rented a cart before the round was over.

Every few minutes we could hear the sound of golf balls ricocheting off a mobile home. The course wound in and around the mobile home park. It didn't take long for us to realize that we wouldn't want our rig parked on or around this golf course. Most of the choice places were already taken. They were the ones that it would be impossible to hit with a golf ball when playing the course. Unless, of course you were a hacker from Nebraska, then you could probably even hit the rigs that were in those choice places. However, the facilities were excellent, very clean and affordable so we would have to put this on our list of places to consider.

We all piled into Norma and Waldo's van and took a tour of the other mobile home parks. Each one of the parks has it's own schedule of events to keep everyone active and busy. Some of them have Executive golf courses, all have their own pools and hot tubs, crafts, games, cards, dances, barbecues, pot luck dinners, and the list goes on and on. You can live in your RV or buy a park model trailer house that sits permanently on your spot. The dealers selling park models advertise that they will take anything in trade that doesn't eat.

I guess that includes our motorhome," Waldo said. "It doesn't eat, but it sure drinks a lot of gasoline."

Chapter Fourteen

IN SEARCH OF A GOLD MINE

Time for us to be moving on if we were going to cover all the territory we had planned on, before we had to return to the cold country! Our plan was to start working our way towards Lake Havasu City, Arizona, where we wanted to investigate a few RV parks and check out the price of real estate.

We pulled our caravan onto Highway 95 heading back towards Quartzsite where we wanted to stop over one more day to see how Pat and Bob were doing in their search for gold. By now they may have already found the mother lode and would be looking for some help to haul it to the bank.

It was warming up fast on that Wednesday morning. The cactus and wildflowers were preparing to burst into bloom. "I sure hope we can stay until the desert blossoms. There has been plenty of rain and soon every cactus will be adorned with sparkling spring colors," I told my mate.

We reached Quartzsite in time to inch our way into the line of traffic we had come to know and expect. This particular morning seemed slower than ever. We heard one man on the CB radio coming in loud and clear, "When we reached the heavy traffic I told my wife to get out and hike to the front of the line to see if she could find a store that sold beer. She found us a six pack, we drank it all, and we still haven't reached the four way stop."

We pulled into the parking area behind the Main Event to see if we could locate Bob and Pat. They were already gone on their motorbikes. A friendly man who was parked next door to them told us they left early that morning, exiting the back way from the parking area. "They've been going out everyday in search of some excitement. They sure are working hard at it. When they come home at night they're exhausted."

"I knew it, they've found gold. We gotta go find 'em, they probably need help carryin' it all in," Dick said.

We loaded into the back of the pickup and found our way in and around the many motorhomes strewn aimlessly in the desert area behind the Main Event. There were

several boondockers parked by themselves, far
enough out so they wouldn't be bothered by
all the noise and excitement of senior
citizens having a good time. There was one
old blue school bus with two Volkswagen vans
welded on top of it.

"Why don't we stop and ask these people
if we can look inside?" I asked. "I've never
seen a two story nest. Maybe we'd fall in
love with it, then you guys could build us a
top story on our motorhome. We could use it
for storage for all the bargains we find at
the swap meets. There might even be room for
my rocking chair. I know where there are
some old vans."

"We're not stopping, we have to find Bob
and Pat before they let someone else in on
their gold mine and we lose out," Dick said.
"Bill, did you bring your metal detector?"

"I brought both of ours, you can use
Beryl's," Bill answered. "We also brought
the dry washer, that'll keep the girls busy.
They can scoop the sand onto the washer after
we find the prime locations with our metal
detectors."

"I can already see that this is bound to
be one of the highlights of our trip. We
brought our golf clubs so if you guys don't
find any gold we're going to set up a golf
course out here in the desert. I've always
wondered what it would be like to play on
sand greens," Beverly said.

We were riding in the back of the pickup,
letting our hair blow free, wishing we had
brought a pile of pillows because we were now
traveling a bumpy, dusty, washboard road.
Cork wasn't having any mercy on those of us
holding down the rear end of the pickup, as
we were bouncing all over the place. We were
about ready to lose our breakfast as we
experienced a weightless feeling as though
our stomachs were floating.

After rambling around the desert for a

least an hour, the guys decided we must have been given the wrong directions. There wasn't anything out here, the earth was as barren as Cork's bald head. We didn't see anything that even resembled a gold mine.

"You girls are so dumb, gold mines don't just show up out in the desert," Eddie said. "Somebody has to start digging a hole before you can call it a mine. Does anyone have any suggestions as to where to go next?"

"Here comes a man in a jeep, maybe he can tell us where to go to look for gold," Waldo said.

"Good grief, don't tell him we're looking for gold. Just tell him we're lost and see if he knows a way out of here without going back the way we came," John said. "The girls are choking to death in the back of the pickup."

We stopped and talked to a man named George Weeks. He told us he owned a small claim another three miles along this dusty road. He does a little bit of mining each day. "It gives me something to do to get out of the house and out of mama's way for a while. We can't drywash in the heat of the summer so I try to accomplish all I can in the winter time. I don't find much, but just a little nugget once in a while keeps me coming back. Follow me if you want to get back onto the Interstate," he said.

"I told you guys to sign up for the Modern Goldminer's Treasure Hunter's Association seminars last week. If you had done that we'd know where to look for our gold mine," LaVern said.

"I know how to get to the New 49er claims, maybe we can look around there. Let's go find out," Bill said.

We found a road on the south side of Interstate 10 and headed towards Dome Rock, west of Quartzsite. The sand and dirt spiraled up around us as we lumbered along the bumpy road. We tried to remember the preacher's words last Sunday when he quoted Phillipians 4:11, "I have learned in whatever state I am to be content."

"Next time the guys can go prospecting by themselves," Margaret said. "We can go to a swap meet or something more exciting than this."

We continued along the road for another five miles climbing steadily towards the mountains. All of a sudden we spotted Pat and Bob coming down a hill off to the west. "We've really found a good place to dry wash. It's off the road a ways, come on I'll show you," Bob said.

We just thought the first road was bumpy. This bike trail was worse than the pasture trails we have to travel at home when we go to fix someone's water well. We soon arrived at a point where we were told we would have to walk for another mile.

"You girls haul the dry washer and the pick and shovels, Bill and I have the metal detectors," Dick said. "Maybe you can get the other guys to help carry it, and don't forget the lunch and water."

"What lunch and what water? We didn't bring anything except ourselves. You didn't tell us we were going on an all day hike. Maybe we'll find a McDonald's further up this trail road," Norma said.

"Now I know why prospectors had donkeys," I said. "I read an article last week that said, 'brains, brawn, beans and burros were the four cardinal essentials of the American prospector. For more than a century, burro and man shared thirst and hunger. Together they endured the desert's scorching days and lonely nights.' Our guys expect us to haul all this stuff up the side of this mountain. Do they plan on using us as their jackass? They may think they have brains and brawn, but the way I see it they're short on beans and a burro, so they better start figuring out how to use their brawn because we just may go on strike," I said.

In this same article about the burros it said, "Old-timers who spent a considerable amount of time with the burro during their gold prospecting days, chose a burro the same way they chose a wife, close your eyes and put your trust in God."

"We can be just like the burro; a lazy, stubborn, tough, unpredictable beast, but faithful," LaVern said.

"You girls know we wouldn't make you carry all this stuff yourself, we'll be right here behind you to goose you if you need it," John said.

The guys helped us carry the drywasher and the other equipment and we soon reached our destination. "Try out the metal detectors right here to the left of this old abandoned mine," Bob told Dick. "You girls get the drywasher set up and we'll soon be in business."

"I read some place that you're not supposed to mess around abandoned mines," Beverly told Dick. "You can get caught in a rock slide inside there, and we would never be able to get you out."

"I found a nugget right here in this crevice outside the mine, we're not going inside. We're going to dig right here," Bob said.

We were all startled by a mellow whistle. It was a pert little bird perched on top of a rock. He had a tawny, cinnamon-colored breast gleaming in the sun, almost like a small robin. Then we could see the nest on a cliff over to the right of where the guys were poking around. The female bird was babysitting the eggs, or the little birds, we couldn't tell which for sure. We don't have birds like this in Nebraska, so it was fascinating to watch.

    "Does   anyone know what kind of bird this
is?" Waldo asked.   "I   didn't   know   we were
going bird watching today."
    "It's a Say's Phoebe," Lavern   told   him.
"You   watch   and see if he catches a fly or a
bug.   If   it's   a   Say's   Phoebe,   they   are
flycatchers.   They   may   also   try and attack
the   men   if   they get too close to the nest.
Let's sit down and watch the action."
    "If you girls didn't   bring any water you
better start building a still," Bill told us.
"All you will need is a bucket and a piece of
clear plastic about   four feet long.   There's
a bucket   and   a   sheet   of   plastic   in   the
pickup.   Somebody   can   go fetch it while the
rest start digging.   Dig   a   hole   about two
feet   deep and three feet wide   at   the   top.
Put the bucket in the hole and cover the hole
with the plastic   and push down the middle to
form a cone.   Seal the plastic   with dirt all
the   way   around   and   we will   soon have some
water.   It will take all   day   to   produce   a
quart of water, so you better get busy."

There was some mumbling and grumbling, but we finally decided we should get started digging because the sun was beating down and the sweat was pouring off the guys as they were in hot pursuit of a vein of gold.

What are we going to do with this gold when we find it?" Norma wanted to know.

"We're going to put it in the till for our retirement center, which we plan to name 'Nebraska Winter Headquarters', Eddie told her. "We may decide here on this mountain would be a good place for our mobile home park that way we'll be close to our gold mine."

"It is beautiful up here, you can look forever and sit and watch all the creatures of the desert coming and going," Pat said.

Beverly was digging in the hole and had it about half as deep as we needed when a big lizard jumped down in the hole with her. She screamed and bolted out of the hole and started running down the hill. "It's just a large Desert Iguana, he won't hurt you if you don't mess with him. You're probably digging around where his home is, he just wants to scare you away. Usually they are scared of people," Bill said.

"Like the Snowbird, the Desert Iguana is a heavy-bodied creature. He also has a long tail and a short snout. He has an overall light-colored appearance and is sometimes called the white lizard. They can grow up to 16 inches, but this one is just a baby, he's only a foot long," Beryl said.

"It's O.K., Beverly, you can come back now," Beryl hollered as she reached down in the hole with a shovel and threw him out. "They like to eat the flowers of the cactus and can do a lot of damage to the cactus by chewing on them."

"I'd like to put him in a box and ship him home to my grandsons. They'd like to

play with him," I said, as I took my turn at
digging. "Should we be drywashing this dirt
we're digging out of here?" I asked. "Let's
do it, we may find gold before the guys do."
 We had a regular system set up, taking turns
digging and scooping the sandy dirt onto the
drywasher. The sweat was rolling off of us,
mixing with the dirt and sand that already
had us covered.

"Women aren't supposed to sweat, they
glisten," Norma said.

"You may not sweat, but I do. Mud is
pouring off me. One thing for sure we'll all
smell the same," Margaret said.

"I wish we had some water, I think I'm
getting dehydrated," LaVern said.

"The worst thing we can do is panic. If
you feel anxiety coming on you need to calm
yourself before it reaches the panic stage.
If one person in the group panics, it will
spread rapidly through the whole group. I'll
be the leader and tell each of you what to do
if you become anxious," Beryl said.
"LaVern, you should find a shady place and
lay down with your feet elevated, and think
of ways you can help yourself. And while
you're laying there think of ways to help the
rest of us, too. I read this in Chuck
Busby's column in the Quartzsite Gem, the
local newspaper."

"How can I lay down when there isn't
anything but rocks and dirt. What if one of
those lizards crawls on me?" LaVern wanted to
know. "If they do you'll see what panic
really is!"

We were all starting to get tired, hot,
dirty, disgusted, and thirsty, when all of a
sudden Norma shouted, "Here's a nugget, look
we've found gold!" Of course, everyone
rushed over to the drywasher to see for
themselves.

"I think it's fool's gold," Cork said.
"No, it isn't," Beryl said. "I've seen

gold nuggets and it's the real thing. Bring
the metal detector."

"Sure enough, it's the real thing," Bill
said as the metal detector started sounding
off.

"I told you there was gold here. I found
a nugget yesterday but this one is bigger,"
Bob said.

Our nugget was about half the size of my
little fingernail. We kept digging in that
spot as Bill came over with his metal
detector and started going over all the dirt
we were throwing out. By this time we were
all searching with whatever we could find to
dig with. We looked like a bunch of dogs
trying to dig out under a fence.

"I think somebody should make a trip back
to town and bring us some food and water, but
don't let anyone know that we've found gold
or we'll have people all over us. We'll know
by tomorrow if we want to stake a claim
here," Bill said.

"Why don't you girls go to town and get
some supplies? We'll stay right here all
night and keep looking. I'm sure we're close
to a big one," Bob said.

"No way! This is our hole and we're not
leaving this spot, you guys go to town for
supplies. Maybe you could bring back the van
or one of the motorhomes. Somebody might get
tired and want to sleep tonight, but I'm
staying right here with this hole. I want to
be here when we find the big vein," I said.

"I'll go for water," Cork said. "Does
anyone want to go along?" Cork, Waldo and
Eddie went to town to bring back all the
supplies we might need to survive the night
and another day in the desert.

It wasn't long until we were all getting
tired of digging and starting to get
dehydrated. I started looking for the shady
spot LaVern had found earlier. I was
wandering around gazing at the different

kinds of cactus when I almost stepped on a
rattlesnake. "Aaaagh!" I screamed as my
heart leaped into my throat. I started
backing up right over the top of a jumping
cactus. I don't know if it reached out and
grabbed me or if I fell into the middle of
it. I kept screaming until help came and
then I screamed some more.

Bill and Bob killed the rattlesnake with
a shovel, but I couldn't quit screaming.
"Whose idea was this anyhow? Oh! Pulleez!
Someone come and Heeellp me!"

Norma borrowed a pair of needle-nosed
pliers from Bob, sat down on a rock, laid me
across her lap and spent the next hour
pulling sixteen spines from my backside.
"OOHH! I think it would have been easier to
let the snake bite me," I cried, as the tears

poured down my face into the sand. I watched as three different cactus reached out to grab my tears before they hit the ground.

"You won't be able to sit for a week," Norma said. "You'll need more than a pillow to sit on when we start our trek down this mountain in that pickup."

I thought about Phillipians 4:11 and started repeating it over and over as I cried. "Dear God, teach me to be content in whatever state I'm in." The Apostle Paul wrote these words in a letter to the Phillipians, after he had been thrown in prison. "At this point I think being in prison would be easier than landing on a cholla cactus," I wailed. "I don't think it's a teddy bear cholla either! Does anyone have any aspirin or pain killer of any kind?"

"I've got a pint of Old Crow in the saddle bag of my bike," Bob said. "Would you like that for pain killer?"

"Yeah, I'll take it, but not to drink. Norma pour it on me, will you please?"

I soon reached a state of calmness and proceeded to walk around so that I wouldn't get stiff all over. I even took my turn again at digging. By this time we had a six foot hole dug and were starting to make it wider. So far there hadn't been any big nuggets of gold, but we had found one more very small one.

When the guys arrived with food and water, we had a picnic in the desert. They had miscounted, thinking there were only eight of us. We learned what it was like to share a McDonald's meal with a bunch of dirty, hungry, desert rats.

"Pass the water please," LaVern said. "I've been about to choke."

"I hope you brought plenty of water. Chuck Busby says we need a gallon of water a day for each person when we're in the desert. Did you bring 12 gallons of water so we have enough for tomorrow?" Beryl asked.

"We brought 20 gallons and some beans and jerky for tomorrow's breakfast, or lunch, whatever you want to call it.   We need to make another trip down to the van to bring up some lawn chairs and blankets. We can take turns digging and sleeping in the chairs. We'll probably need someone to guard the area, too. You never know when we might have claim jumpers," Waldo said.

"Since I can't sit down, I'll take the first watch," I said. "What do I do if someone comes up the hill? Scream or cry? I've become pretty good at both in the last hour."

The sun setting over the mountains was a brilliant display of color. I always think of the desert as being dry, drab and dull. The colors of that sunset turned the hills from lavender to deep purple, then a soft turquoise, ending in a restful blue. It was such a calming, serene sight. The stately giant saguaro were silhouetted against the craggy mountain tops. We were sitting there marveling at the beauty when we heard the fist coyote howl.

"Holy cow, I hope there aren't as many as it sounds like," Norma said.

"It sounds like a mother trying to teach her little ones how to howl," Pat said.

"It's just one, that's the way they howl," Cork said.

"Now, what am I supposed to do when I'm standing watch and they decide to attack me? Or I've heard they can lure dogs away from a campsite. What about Beryl's dog?" I asked.

"We'll just keep Poco on a leash, he'll be all right," Beryl said.

"What if he goes back and gathers up all his buddies and tells them about his great find? We're kind of vulnerable sitting out here in the open without any protection.

There's other creatures that come out at night, too. Whose idea was this?" Margaret wanted to know.

"I can just see the headlines in the _Quartzsite Gem_ next week. 'A whole group of Prospectors found in the mountains, dehydrated, starving and chewed up by coyotes'," Beverly said.

By this time it was dark thirty. In Nebraska that means 30 minutes after dark. Bill started telling a story that he had read in Chuck Busby's column in the _Quartzsite Gem_. "There was this cowboy who was well known as a roper, most of the time he roped calves. But one day when riding around in the mountains he ran across a bobcat and so he tried to rope him. It seems the cat wasn't too happy about this and climbed the rope right up to his arm. Every time he'd get the cat off he'd climb right back up his arm until he finally got the rope off of the saddle horn. The cat took off, rope and all. The horse wasn't too happy about this incident either and threw the cowboy into the rocks. Busby said he wasn't too sure whether to believe this tale until the cowboy took off his jacket and rolled up his sleeve. His right arm up past his elbow was nothing but a mass of knotted scars."

"Busby then quoted an old adage that says, 'Everything in the desert either sticks, stings, or bites,' then he added, 'When you go out on the desert don't get in the cholla cactus, don't mess with rattlesnakes, and above all, don't rope bobcats'!"

"That sounds like good advice to me, but you could have told me all of this before I messed with the rattlesnake and sat on a cholla," I told Bill.

"Are there any other creatures we need to know about?" LaVern asked, as the coyotes seemed to be picking up tempo and joining in a chorus. "There must be a dozen of them out there now, I'm starting to get scared."

"If we find a gold mine are we going to have to spend all of our retirement years up here digging holes and drywashing, or are we going to be able to hire all this work done?" Norma wanted to know.

"The way I see it, unless we really find a good vein we're going to have to do all the digging   ourselves.   We   should know by tomorrow at noon whether we want to continue with this or just use it as a place to do some   drywashing   whenever we don't have anything else to do," Bill said.

"Well, I can't sit so I'm going down to the van and lay down on my stomach, does anyone want to walk with me?" I asked.

"What if the coyotes attack us between here and there?   It's a mile back to the van and it's pitch dark," Pat said.

"Come on, I'm not afraid of a little coyote. If these guys had sense enough to get them a burro, he'd keep the coyotes away. In some places the ranchers buy guard donkeys to keep dogs and coyotes away from sheep and cattle. If the donkey catches a coyote, he'll bite it and stomp it to death.   When the guys get the gold mine producing, we'll get them a donkey to keep coyotes away," Beryl said.

The excitement of finding that first nugget seemed to be fading away as the hour grew later. It wasn't long until all the girls were at the van and pickup, fast asleep. But, the guys were determined, they kept digging.

Chapter Fifteen

PARADISE

It was 8 a.m. when I awoke the next morning. The night had been cool, but already the sun was pouring in through the windows and our sweaty, dirty bodies were attracting all kinds of buzzing insects. I tried to move and found it impossible as my backside was swollen and bruised. I smelled like I'd been on a 10 day drunk as the combination of Old Crow, encrusted dirt and sweat was almost nauseating.

"I'm sure I'll never be able to sit again," I moaned, bringing my friends out of their half-conscious state into what we had been led to believe would some day be our own version of Paradise. In order to finance our Paradise we were placing a lot of importance on finding a gold mine.

"This is worse than waiting on an oil well to come in," LaVern said.

"Let's take the beans and jerky up to the men and see how they're doing with our gold mine," Pat said.

"We're each supposed to get one gallon of water a day. I don't know whether to wash my face with mine, or pour it in a hole and sit in it," I said. "Wouldn't a hot tub feel good right now?"

"I can't function until after I've had my morning coffee," Norma said. "If I have a

caffeine fit everybody will know it. Maybe
cactus roots would make good coffee. Let's
start a fire and find out. On second
thought, I can wait till the sun gets hotter
and the water will probably boil without a
fire. It's only February, can you imagine
what it would be like here in July?" she
asked.

"We can't waste our water on any of those
things. It's already getting hot, and we'll
need it to drink. There are only two buckets
left. We'll take one five gallon bucket to
the men and leave the other one here. Get
the beans and jerky and let's go," Beryl
said.

"Boy, that Beryl's a slave driver. I
wish we had some bacon and eggs. We all like
beans, but I didn't think I'd be eating them
for breakfast," Beverly said.

"Where are we going to go to the bathroom
in the daylight?" Margaret asked. "It wasn't
so bad last night after dark. The tissue I
had along is all gone, what are we supposed
to use for toilet paper? I've even used all
the leftover McDonald's napkins."

"You just squat behind a greasewood bush
or a Palo Verde tree," Pat answered. "This
is what you call roughing it."

"I don't mind squatting behind a tree,
but I have to have some toilet paper. Going
without is worse than using corn cobs.
That's what I call roughing it," Margaret
replied.

The mile uphill, between the van and the
potential gold mine, was getting longer each
time I had to climb it, as I lumbered along
at a painful gait. When we arrived at the
excavation site, half of the gold miners were
snoring in the lawn chairs while the other
three were still digging away like a whirly
gust of woodpeckers.

"You girls are just in time. We sure do
need a rest. I know we're close to hitting

the big one," Cork said.

"Have you found any more big nuggets?" Margaret wanted to know.

"No, but we've been panning some of the finer sand and we're sure there's gold in it. We've got a pickup load to take back to town to pan out. Either that or we have to haul water up here," Dick said.

"How are we going to get all that pile of dirt down to the pickup?" Beryl asked.

"When our buckets are empty we're going to haul it down the hill one bucket at a time," Eddie said. "You girls can start by filling the two empty buckets with the dirt that's left after we drywashed all the big rocks out. And, while you're down at the van, bring back the whisk broom. We want to sweep up every bit of fine sand that's laying around here."

"If you guys had a burro you'd at least feed him before you asked him to make a trip down the mountain. Let's eat breakfast first," I said.

"We don't have a can opener for the beans. How are we going to eat them?" LaVern asked.

John pulled out his pocket knife and opened the cans of beans. We used our dirty plastic silverware left over from the McDonald's banquet the night before. We all drank our fill of water like it might be the last we would ever get.

After breakfast John cut the tops out of the two plastic buckets that had been emptied of water and we girls started filling them with the dirt and sand to be panned. Bev, Norma, Beryl and I made the first trip to the pickup. We took turns carrying, but it was still a heavy load.

"Brains, brawn, beans, and burros," I kept repeating as the rocks and dirt scrunched underneath our heavy load. "It seems to me like the guys have the brains and

beans and we're the brawn and the burro. How
much is gold worth anyhow? I'm not sure this
is going to be a profitable venture."
   "It was $357.50 a troy ounce last time I
checked," Beryl said. "As heavy as these
buckets are they must be solid gold."
   "Wow, that's a lot of money for an ounce
of gold," Norma said, "Now I know why we're
hauling buckets of dirt up and down the
mountain. I was beginning to wonder if we
were crazy."
   The stench that surrounded us reminded me
of something our son Jerry said to our eight
year old grandson, Mitchell, after he'd
spilled his food all over himself for the
third time. "Have you ever wondered why the
flies follow you around, or why the pigs wink
at you every time you pass by, or why the
girls run the other way when they see you
coming?"
   "Let's make one more trip, then go on
strike until they buy us a burro. We can set
up a golf course out here and play golf while
the men haul the dirt. This is not my idea
of a vacation or a pleasant way to spend our
retirement either," Beverly said.
   "Before we come back next year I'm going
to check with Clyde Cox, who lives across the
road from us, he's got two mama burros and
three babies. One of them had twins," I
said. "They ought to be just the right size
next year. We can pull a horse trailer
behind the motorhome next winter instead of
our car. We probably won't need a car if
we're going to spend all our time gold
mining."
   It took us an hour to make the trip down
the hill and back up, then we sat down on a
rock to rest. "My tail's still too sore to
sit, so I'm going back down to the van. I'm
ready to do something different. I'll make
up the rules and set up the course for the
golf game," I told them as I started walking

back to the van.

"I'll carry a bucket down as I go," Margaret said. "I'm ready to play golf, too. We're going to be just like a burro...strong, tough, healthy and spirited. We're balking. You guys can haul the rest of the dirt."

Quartzsite has a golf course called Greasewood Greens. There is nothing on the course that is green. In last year's **Quartzsite Nugget**, a special paper put out by the Palo Verde Valley Times, there was an article about the golf course. "It's not Torrey Pines or Pebble Beach, but to Quartzsite residents and visitors, Greasewood Greens Golf Course is a true challenge." It costs a total of three dollars to play the nine hole course where divots are rare and the greens are sand. As a matter of fact, the whole course is sand. They boast of having 10 players a day during the busy winter season. During the Pow Wow the course is used for a parking area for more RV's, so there's no way you can get a tee time.

As we walked back down the hill for the umpteenth time, we started talking about the rules we would need in order to play, and how we were going to set the course up in the desert.

"I think it'd be best to have the greens down in the washes, that'll be the sandiest place," Norma said.

"We want the course to be a challenge so let's start hole #1 right here by the van and run it up this hill, then fix a dogleg back down into the wash," LaVern suggested.

"From there we can run hole #2 up that steep mountain side and then around by the canyon and into the wash on the other side," Margaret said. "We don't want it to be too easy, or it won't be worth the bother."

"Hole #3 should be a short hole, we can put the tee box right there beside where the guys are digging. This will be the only hole

that   doesn't have the green in the wash."   I
said.   "If we're lucky   we   can   ricochet the
ball off of that boulder and   right   into the
hole."

     "Hole #4   will   be   a long one, straight
down the mountain   with the green in the wash
close by the van.   We can stop at the van and
take   a   nap as we go by," Bev said.   "By the
way how are we going to lug our clubs?"

     "We could use a couple of golf carts, but
I don't see any around here.   Matter   of fact
we   don't even have any pull carts.   We can't
let the guys think   we're weaklings.   I don't
think these clubs are any heavier than a five
gallon   bucket   of   dirt, so let's just carry
them," Beryl said.

Tee time in the desert

Rules for golf on the desert:

1. Play winter rules. You can set your ball up on anything you can find.
2. If your ball hits a saguaro cactus it's a two stroke penalty. We must protect the saguaro at all times.
3. If a rattlesnake, desert iguana, or kangaroo rat swallows your ball, you have to hit it anyway.
4. Be sure you rake the greens after each hole. If you don't have a rake lay down on the green, on your back, and wave your arms and legs in the manner you would if making a snow angel. That should smooth all the foot prints. Large indentations left by your backside are O.K.
5. In case of a Desert Storm, suspend play until we can contact "Stormin" Norman Schwarzkopf for further instructions.
6. If your ball lands in a cholla cactus, you can reach in and get it if you want to, but the smart thing to do is play another ball, with one stroke penalty. Anyone who gets cholla spines in them will be penalized one stroke for each spine, and if necessary, disqualified for delay of game.
7. The only out of bounds on the course is the excavation area where the guys are eagerly hunting for gold. They are not to be disturbed for any reason.
8. Rattlesnakes shorter than driver length may be dropped away from. Longer ones will probably swallow your ball, in which case refer to rule #3.
9. Mating rattlesnakes are to be treated the same as any other species. Leave them alone and let them enjoy.
10. If you still want to play golf after reading these rules you are really desperate. Above all else have fun and enjoy the game.

Pat had never played golf before, but we
assured her the only thing necessary for
playing this course was a matching outfit.
"It doesn't matter whether you can hit the
ball or not, if you look like a golfer that's
all that's necessary," LaVern told her.
"See, we all have on matching outfits.
They're so dirty you can't see what color
they are. You can always pick the ball up
and throw it. We just play for fun, we're
not out for blood. Sometimes we do a little
gambling with our game, but you won't lose
any more than your share in the gold mine."

We played two threesomes so that we could
keep the play moving along smoothly. Very
important on any golf course. "I can't
believe we're doing this after complaining
about carrying those buckets of dirt. These
clubs are breaking my shoulders. I never
walk and carry my clubs at home, I don't even
like to walk!" Norma said.

"Well, this is the only course we have
right now so we'll just have to adjust. We
drove over to Blythe once to see if we could
get on the course there, and they had people
stacked on top of people waiting for tee
times. We don't have time to wait around
like that, our vacation is getting shorter
and besides, we might lose a couple of pounds
doing this," I told them as everyone was
moaning, groaning, sweating, huffing and
puffing.

When we arrived on top of the hill, where
the guys were busy carrying buckets of gold
dust back and forth to the pickup, they
informed us they only had two more trips to
make and would soon be ready to join us in a
round of golf.

The sky was turning grey and started
rumbling as we teed off on the fourth hole.
"Maybe we'll get some rain, I could sure use
a shower right now," Bob said as he passed us
trudging down the hill.

The wind started howling at hurricane speed and it wasn't long until the hills turned grey as the sand dunes started migrating northward.   "Is this when we suspend play and call for Stormin' Norman?" Pat wanted to know. Then the rain started pouring down.

"Oh! Isn't this heavenly," I said, as I dropped my clubs and lifted my head to allow the rain to roll down my cheeks, leaving streaks of mud.

"We do have to finish this hole, you know," Beryl said.   "The guys will be ready to join us by the time we reach the bottom of the hill. As long as there isn't any lightning we can't suspend play."

We finished out the hole and stopped at the van to see if the men wanted to play our little four hole course.   "We'll have to share our clubs with them because they didn't bring theirs.   They can be our caddies," Beverly said.   "Now we can have three foursomes."

We succeeded in lining everyone up so they had partners and started our long awaited golf game. The sky was turning as black as coal and the rain continued to pour down, but it felt great so we didn't pay any attention to it. Just as the first group had approached #2 green Bill looked up and hollered. "Heeey! Get out of the wash there's a wall of water coming!"   Everybody scrambled out of the wash and we looked up just in time to see our sand greens floating down the wash.

"So that's what you were talking about when you said stay away from the washes when it rains," I said.   "If I could swim I'd jump in, that water looks marvelous.   Does anyone have any soap?"

"Let's get to the pickup and see if we can find a way out of here without driving through a wash, we may have to find a high

spot   and   stay   there until the rain stops,"
Beryl said.
     When we arrived at the pickup the dirt we
had hauled down the hill was   turning   to mud
and   was   in   danger of floating out onto the
ground. "Cover   the   pickup   with   that   big
piece of plastic the girls were   going to use
to   make a still," Bill said. "We don't want
to lose any of that gold."
     We waited around for about an hour until
the   rain   let up and the low   clouds   rolled
aside,   revealing   a   patch of blue sky and a
piercing   ray of   sunshine.   Then   we   piled
eight stinking, wet bodies into   the   van and
started our trek out of the desert.
     While   we   were   driving along, following
two of the guys in the pickup and Bob and Pat
on their motorbikes, three antelope came from
nowhere   and   started racing us down the dirt
road.   "I   think   they're   pronghorns"   Bill
said.   "They're   a   cinnamon-buff color   with
black   horns.   The horns are shed every year
because they're   hollow.   The   pronghorn   is
another   species of the desert   that   doesn't
have to have water.   The article I read about
them said they   like to run along beside cars
and can run 35 miles an hour."
     "Well, one thing for sure we've learned a
lot about the creatures of the desert on this
trip, whether   we   learned   anything   else or
not," Waldo said.
     It seemed like we had been in   the desert
for two weeks instead of two days.   Everybody
was tired, weary and stinky, but the men were
determined to continue the hunt for gold.
     "This   dirt is already wet,   let's   start
panning   it to see if we want to invest money
in a gold mine," Bob said.
     "I can hardly wait   to find some place to
take a shower.   Why don't we drive on over to
Lake   Havasu yet this afternoon and see if we
can   find a campground?   I've   had   all   the
desert and gold mining I can   handle for this

trip," LaVern said.

"I'm going in my motorhome and take a shower, there isn't any reason why we can't, we'll be at a campground with full hookups tonight or tomorrow. I don't care if I use every drop of water we have. Then I'm going over to the Main Event Restaurant and order me a big steak," I said.

"That's the smartest idea I've heard all day," Beverly said, with Pat and Beryl agreeing.

"Wait for me, I'm coming too," Norma and Margaret both hollered at the same time.

I did try to ration the water so my mate could have a shower, too. It took quite awhile to wash all the sand out of my hair and out of the bottom of the shower. What a refreshing feeling to know you smell good again. My wet clothes still reeked of alcohol, sweat, tears and blood. The laundromat would be our first destination after the shower room when we arrived in Lake Havasu City. The men spent the rest of the afternoon panning for gold. They carried water from a hydrant near by. We brought them some dinner and they worked until about 8 p.m. They did find some fine dust, so Bob was going to see about staking a claim. "This way we'll have a place to do a little dry washing when we come back next year," Bob said. "For all we know, someone else may already have a claim there."

"We've decided to let Bob have his gold mine back, he can work it awhile to see what develops," Dick said. "At least we've had our exercise these last few days."

"There could still be a good vein there some place. I think I'd enjoy coming back next year and searching for more gold," John said.

"Some people stumble onto gold mines accidently and some have to work for every little bit they can scrounge up. I heard a

neat   story   the other day," Bob said.   "Back
in   the 1900s   six   men   were   attending   the
burial   of a friend.   The men   were   kneeling
around   the   freshly   dug   grave   while   the
preacher was telling   them what a fine guy he
had been.   One man began to examine the earth
he   was   kneeling on.   He found it thick with
gold.   The news moved   fast   from   one man to
the other.   The preacher soon   caught   on and
shouted,   'Gold!   You're   all dismissed!'   The
body   was   moved   to   another   site   and   the
digging began."

 We   spent the night there in the   parking
area   behind   the   Main   Event.   Cork took a
shower, using all   the water we had left.   We
both   fell into bed exhausted,   but   couldn't
get   to   sleep.   "When   I look back over the
last few days I   can't   believe we went crazy
over the possibility of finding   gold," Cork
said.   "You'd have thought we were a bunch of
money-hungry mongrels," he added.

 "Does money have   to be that important to
us?   Can   we really find Paradise   by   being
rich?   I   don't   think so.   All the money in
the world won't   buy   us a place in Paradise.
We were carrying those buckets   of   dirt down
that   hill   as if we thought Paradise could be
carried in a bucket.   What really is our idea
of   Paradise?   What are we really   searching
for?" I asked.

 "My   idea   of   Paradise   is being able to
retire, with you   by my side, wherever it may
be," he answered.   "To have good   health, and
to   be able to travel anywhere we want in our
motorhome.   To see the many things and places
we   haven't seen before we get   too   old   and
crippled   to enjoy them.   And then, to find a
place here in this   warm country for a winter
home."

 "To that I could add only these   things,"
I said.   "I pray that we will take God as our
co-pilot wherever   we   go,   the   Bible as our
guide, and Jesus as our Saviour.   To let God

lead us and guide us through each day we have
left of our lives, and to spend some time
each day doing something for others. That's
how I think we will find our way to Paradise.
And last, that .we find a delightful, plush,
golf course at every stop on our journey.
Good night, dear."
    "Good night, sleep tight."

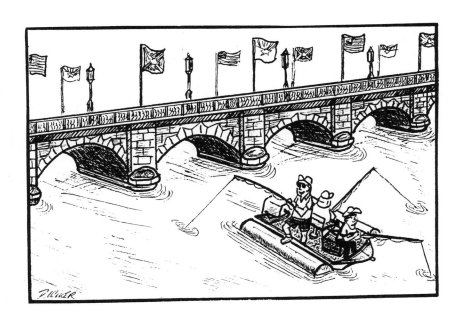

Chapter Sixteen

THE COLORADO RIVER &
LAKE HAVASU CITY

We rolled out of bed early, anxious to move on to another adventure. I opened the window in the motorhome and a sweet rush of warm, yeasty air hit me right in the nostrils. The spicy fragrance of raisins, buttered nuts and drizzled, powdered sugar frosting was heavenly. "They're cooking up a fresh batch of cinnamon rolls over at the

Main Event. Wouldn't you like to have a nice, big, fat one for breakfast?" I asked my mate.

"No, I wouldn't. You don't need one either. Have you looked at your backside lately?"

"As a matter of fact I have. It still hurts and I thought a scrumptious cinnamon roll would make it feel better," I answered in a pouty way.

"The only thing it will do is make you grow bigger. Let's have our cereal and forget the goodies."

"Whatever you say, dear."

Our group was gathered ready to head north to Parker and Lake Havasu City. We wanted to find the Colorado River and try our luck at fishing, and see if there wasn't a better golf course somewhere on this desert. We were still searching for the ideal place for retirement.

On a bright, sunshiny morning we pulled into the line of traffic only to find it hadn't improved any from the week before. We inched our way to the four-way stop at the speed of an arthritic turtle. It only took an hour to make our way through town and head north on Highway 95.

We were approaching the edge of town when I noticed a covey of quail. "Look!" I squealed, "aren't they beautiful? I bet they are the desert Gambels Quail. The desert quail has a white, unscaled belly. They are equipped to survive the desert's hostile environment. See the teardrop-shaped top knot, and light brown-colored crown."

"I was reading about them just the other day," Cork said. In the winter time they form coveys of 20 to 100. They break up into pairs during February and March for mating and nesting. See, it is mating season!"

North of Quartzsite on Highway 95 is the city's landfill. They have a free sewer dump

and there were only 12 rigs lined up waiting
their turn to dump.   We were planning on
being in an RV park that evening so opted not
to wait in line.
     The Colorado River was a welcome sight
after spending several days on the desert.
The river winds in and around the city of
Parker, with condominiums, RV resorts,
motels, and campgrounds woven into the
landscape. It was plain to see that Parker
is a resort area where Snowbirds and people
of all ages come to play. There is beach-
side camping at several State Park sites on
the California side of the river.

LaVern came on the CB, "They have a great golf course here called Emerald Canyon, we played it last year. It's lots of fun and I think you would all enjoy it, but let's find a place to park first, we can come back here later. Watch for it on both sides of the highway as we drive through."

"If you feel like a mountain goat, we can stop at Havasu Spring's Resort," John said. "You have to have lots of golf balls when you play this course, cause it's a doozy. They have a big campground, but this time of year they're always full. It's on the left after we pass Parker Dam."

We traveled on to Lake Havasu with part of us choosing the Crazy Horse Campground. John and LaVern and Norma and Waldo wanted to try out a new park called the Islander RV Resort. Crazy Horse is built on three levels, with the Snowbirds who come to stay all winter parking on the upper levels close to the recreation room, laundry and showers. We were ushered to the lower level, by the beach, where the only hookup we could get was electricity. We spent the rest of the day lolling in a chaise lounge along the Mediterranean-blue water, watching Snowbirds play.

"Some of those old guys can really water ski," Eddie said. "I figured I was getting too old for that, but maybe not. We'll have to give it a try."

"I thought it would be fun to go parasailing. Is anyone else interested? That's where you wear a parachute and they pull you on skis behind the boat and you go flying up into the air. Doesn't that sound like fun? Another thing they do over at Lake Meade is bungee jumping. That's where you tie big rubber bands around your ankles and jump off the cliff towards the water, but the rubber bands grab you before you reach the water. Then you bounce and bounce upside

down, hanging by your ankles.   I think that
would be really exciting, don't you?"

"My   ideas   of   excitement   are   somewhat
different from yours," Beverly said. "I just
want to sit here and rest.   The   last
excitement we got into has tired me out."

We watched the vibrant, crimson sun slip
over the craggy mountain tops and stayed
there   in   the   calm,   breezeless   evening
listening to the water lapping against the
shore. Then it was exciting to see the full
moon peek over the mountains to the east.

"Watching   that   big   harvest   moon   makes
even an old man get romantic ideas," Bill
said. "It really is Snowbird Mating Season.
Come on grandma, let's go to bed."

"This is a beautiful view, but I think we
picked the wrong place," I told my mate. "I
bet the Islander has a swimming pool and a
hot tub. I could soak my sore buns. I make
a motion we get up early in the morning and
see if they have any openings at the
Islander." I talked my husband into moving,
but Beryl and Bill and Bev and Dick chose to
stay on at the Crazy Horse Campground.

At 8 a.m. we were waiting in line for a
parking place. If someone moved out we would
get a spot, if they didn't we would have to
turn around and go back to Crazy Horse. We
waited in line for about an hour and the wait
was well worth it.   "This is what I call
first class accommodations," Cork said.
There were two swimming pools, two hot tubs,
nature trails, boat ramp, a picnic area,
horseshoe pits, and shuffleboard courts.
Activities   included   square,   round   and
ballroom dancing,   live   entertainment,
exercise classes, arts and crafts, bingo,
card games, pot lucks, pancake breakfasts,
and ice cream socials. The clubhouse had a
convenience store, rest rooms and showers,
laundromat, library, card room, billiards, TV
room, arts and crafts room, workshop and a

recreation hall with dance floor.

Our first goal was to shop around town looking over the many options that were available to the average Snowbird who comes to Lake Havasu for the winter. We stopped by the Chamber of Commerce and picked up literature about the city and all the activities that were scheduled. The staff was very friendly and anxious to tell us about their city.

Betsey Hoyt, Public Relations Manager, and Brenda Samchuck, director of the Chamber, explained the story of their city and about the London Bridge.

"Lake Havasu has a year round population of 25,000. 1.5 million people vacation in this modern metropolis every year. The lake has sometimes been described as 'A Lake On The Moon'. Lake Havasu is the focal point for a modern day resort, with dark mountains, ruggedly hugging the shore and only mesquite and cacti to relieve the dry, desert terrain which forms the lake's banks. Lush green golf courses, colorful gardens, a desert teaming with life and, of course, the lake forms the setting that draws vacationers to Lake Havasu City each year," Betsey explained.

The London Bridge was fascinating to us as we read about the history of the bridge. On June 15, 1825, the first stone was laid by the Lord Mayor of London, John Garratt. The bridge over the Thames River was built out of granite which was quarried on Dartmoor. It was a structure of five arches with overall dimensions of 928 feet long and 49 feet wide. The bridge was opened six years later. In 1962 it was discovered that the London Bridge was falling down, sinking into the Thames because it was not adequate for the increase in traffic. Robert McCulloch learned that the British Government was putting the bridge up for sale. He submitted the winning bid of

$2,460,000.

Plans were made to move and reconstruct the bridge in Lake Havasu City, Arizona. Each piece was marked with four numbers. The bridge was shipped by boat 10,000 miles to Long Beach, California. From there it was trucked to Lake Havasu City. On September 23, 1968, the Lord Mayor of London, Sir Gilbert Inglefield, laid the corner stone. A civil engineer from Nottingham, England, was in charge of the reconstruction of the London Bridge in Lake Havasu. The bridge was completed and dedicated on October 10, 1971.

The city celebrates London Bridge Days with a week long festival each year in October. Lake Havasu grew in leaps and bounds as business and residential buildings started sprouting up everywhere. The London Bridge, with the English Village under its arches, creates a pleasing, old-world atmosphere. Visitors and local residents alike enjoy browsing through the more than 50 shops and eateries of the English Village. The Village is open 365 days a year.

"There is something here for everyone," Betsey said. "There are fishing tournaments, world-class boat races, and model sea plane competitions. Nature lovers are enthralled with the wonders in nearby wildlife refuges, touring through the desert by jeep or on foot, or taking a boat tour through scenery made to marvel at, where no car can go. You can visit ghost towns from mining and pioneer days. We have arts and craft shows, galleries to browse in, dinner theaters, concerts to attend and festivals of all kinds. You can ride a shuttle bus to Laughlin or take a cruise on the Dixie Belle, a replica of an old southern stern-wheeler. If you have a group that wants to rent a boat and do your own exploring of the lake and the Colorado River, there are places that can fix you up with a house boat, or you can go wind surfing, sailboating, canoeing, parasailing, or take a jet boat tour."

"If water sports aren't your bag, you can golf on one of our three 18 hole courses. The list of activities goes on and on. Oh! don't forget Saturday is our sixth annual Snowbird Jamboree. It's a time when businesses and local residents take time to thank all Snowbirds for choosing Lake Havasu City for their winter home. There will be booths set up where you can sign-up for free prizes. This is all done under the bridge at the English Village. Be sure and come on down, I know you will enjoy it," she said.

"Wow! I think we can find something to do here," Norma said. "Let's get the group together and decide what we want to do first."

"I've always wanted to rent a house boat and cruise up and down the lake and the Colorado River," Bill said. "We could even have our own fishing tournament."

"We have to drive over to Laughlin, at least for one day," Waldo, the gambler in our group, said. "We may even want to drive the motorhomes over there and stay two or three days. We could try it for a day and see if we want to pack up and move over there."

"I've always wanted to drive to Oatman. "It's an old, deserted mining town. They even have wild burros that walk up and down the streets mooching food," LaVern said.

"Maybe we could borrow one of them the next time someone gets the idea to go prospecting," Margaret said.

"We want to play the golf courses at least once. If some of you would rather go fishing, you can rent a small boat, then when we finish golfing we'll rent a big boat so we can all catch the beauty of the lake and the Colorado River," I said.

"We want to have one day just for
shopping and to look the city over," Beverly
said. "I heard they have a factory outlet
mall here. I think we should look at
condominiums, too. We may be ready to give
up the motorhome, buy a condo, hire us a
maid, and sit back and enjoy the luxurious
way of living."

"All in favor of playing golf tomorrow
raise your hands," Beryl said. Eight hands
went up quickly, with four of the guys
agreeing to rent a boat and try their luck at
fishing. The rest of us found out we could
get on the golf course without a tee time at

the Queen's Bay, a London Bridge Resort
course. We quickly called the London Bridge
and Stonebridge courses and made tee times
for the next two days. We were all set. The
Queen's Bay was a challenging 9 hole
executive course. It was just right for
walking, although some of us opted to rent a
cart anyhow, because we were still tired!

"You guys line us up a pontoon boat or a
house boat for the weekend, we'll show you
how to fish. If we catch enough fish we'll
have a fish fry at the Crazy Horse Campground
under the awning of our motorhome," Beryl
said.

"By Monday we should be ready to try our
luck at the slot machines and tables at
Laughlin," Waldo said.

Our schedule was all set and it didn't
take us long to get into the swing of things
on the golf course. That evening we all met
at the Casa De Miguel Restaurant for Mexican
food. It provided an Old Mexico setting with
food to match.

"This town is really fixed up good for
eating places," John said. "We've tried some
of them, but if you're watching your diet,
you better eat at home. They have places
like Hog Heaven, where they serve barbecue;
EZ's Fine Dining, where they make homemade
deep dish pies and desserts; and the Boarding
House at the Pioneer Hotel has a buffet
that's out of this world. They also have
live entertainment in the bar most every
night. We ought to try the Golden Horseshoe
Steakhouse, they have live country western
music every night. If you want something
fancier, there's a whole list of restaurants
just waiting for us to try.

"How many fish did you guys catch today?"
Bev wanted to know.

"If we count the ones that got away the
grand total is three," Bill said. "We
only brought one home."

"We'll be ready for the fish fry before the rest of you even get a chance to fish. We'll probably reel them in two at a time tomorrow," Dick said.

The next two days we enjoyed our golf game on plush greens and fairways. It was best not to venture out of the fairway, or you were playing the type of golf we played in the desert. The London Bridge and Stonebridge courses were both long and challenging. We played all over the course, making sure we received our money's worth. After golf each day we checked out the shopping areas, browsed through the London Bridge Village and the factory outlet stores. We were shown through several condominiums as we debated whether to go the condo route or stay with our RV's. The condos that rested on the sandy shores of Lake Havasu were very inviting. It gave us something to think about in our spare time.

"It's almost time for us to move on, and we haven't even begun to check out everything in this town," Cork said.

Saturday morning we stopped by the London Bridge to find a musical, fun-filled celebration, going on to honor Snowbirds. It wasn't long until we were caught up in the whirlwind of excitement as we joined in a sing-a-long and watched the square dancing and clogging. There was a state banner contest as different states competed for the first prize, which was something we might want to work on for next year. We made our way around to all the booths, signed up for give-a-ways, and ate our fill of ice cream cones and other goodies. Then we walked to the resort boat rentals under the London Bridge where we boarded our pontoon boat.

Bill was our captain, as he had sailed these waters before. He knew where all the fish were supposed to be, how to catch them, and most of all, how to keep us off sandbars and places where we might get high-centered. We found our way to the Crazy Horse campground, launching close to where the motorhomes were so we could load up the fishing supplies. "Don't you girls forget to bring the lunch like you did when we went prospecting," Dick said.

"Don't you worry, we don't go anywhere without packing food and water. Bernita even carried her lunch and a water jug to the golf course. She was afraid we'd get lost in the desert and she'd starve to death," Beverly said. "She even carried a snake bite kit and a pair of needle-nosed pliers."

The name of Lake Havasu is taken from the American Indian words "Haha vasu" meaning blue water. The water was such a calming, restful blue. We spent most of the day trolling up to Parker Dam and pausing now and then to try our luck fishing the deep water for stripers.

Only five of us could fish at one time, two off of each side and one from the back. Most of us girls didn't have a fishing license anyway, but were available for advice, if needed, and sometimes when it wasn't needed. "I can't believe we've fished all day and you guys haven't caught anything. How are we going to have a fish fry?" Norma wanted to know.

Bill, Dick, Waldo and Eddie were all experienced fishermen. They had all been to Canada where they caught mammoth lake trout and walleye. Bill even has a stuffed fish hanging over the fireplace in the family room.

"I caught one bigger than that, but when I was reeling him in Dick reached over and whopped him with the net and knocked him off my line. That's a true fish story," Bill said.

"I heard a good fish story the other day," Waldo said. "This guy was fishing with his buddy and they hadn't caught much all afternoon when Joe felt a tug on his line. He was using a midnight rattle, artificial lure and he hooked and landed two large-mouth bass on the same lure. Fifteen minutes later he felt another tug on his line, only this one was a bigger fish. Much to his surprise, he had hooked two more fish!"

"Maybe you guys ought to use one of those midnight rattlers on your line," LaVern suggested.

"I heard you're supposed to use a fatso lure and trail it with anchovies, or a pig-n-jig," Beryl said. "As soon as it's my turn to fish I'll show you how. I've got a pig-n-jig and I know how to catch big-mouth bass."

"Listen to her! I want to see this. I'll bet I can catch more large mouth bass in the next two hours than you can. We'll start right now," Bill said.

Norma decided she was ready to fish and was going to show the guys how to catch stripers. "This time of year you have to fish deep for stripers," she said. "We can't mess around waiting for these guys to catch us enough fish so we can have a fish fry."

"Someone else can take my place," John said. "I've just been draggin' my line for the last two hours. If you don't bait your hook, you can't catch fish. If you don't catch fish, you don't have to clean them."

Bill caught the first fish, a medium-sized, large-mouth bass. Beryl was just getting warmed up though and it wasn't long till she caught a big one. Waldo and Dick both caught small ones and Beryl pulled another big one into the boat.

"What did you say you were using for bait?" Dick wanted to know. "Why aren't these night crawlers working?"

"You have to have a pig-n-jig," Beryl repeated.

The mosquitos started biting at the same

time the fish did.   Beryl whipped in another
big fish while everyone else was commenting
on the mosquitos. "Up in Canada, where we
went fishing, the mosquitos ate the horses
and were pitching the shoes to see who got
the harness," Eddie said. "Actually the
only time they'll hurt you is when they drop
you."

"Has anyone else been fishing deep for
stripers?" Norma wanted to know.

"Yes, we have, but they're not biting,"
Waldo told her.

"I   have   this   secret   formula that's
guaranteed to catch a fish every time," I
said. "If you want to try it I'll guarantee
it will catch a fish within five minutes.
Norma, do you want to try it?"

"Sure, I'll try anything," she answered.

I walked over to Norma and had her reel
in her line, then I smeared my formula on her
fatso lure and we sat back to wait. Within
two minutes Norma pulled in a big, striped
bass. "OOh! I like this, let's do it again,"
she said. After Norma had landed six big
stripers the guys were coming over wanting to
know what I had put on her lure.

"Are you just using a fatso lure?" Dick
asked.

"That's all except for Bernita's secret
formula. Maybe if you ask, she'll give you
some, too."

"O.K. smarty, what are you using, we want
to catch some of these big ones, too?" Dick
said.

"It's hemorrhoid ointment, you want
some?"

"Why   would   fish   like hemorrhoid
ointment?"

"Well, I hate to give away my secret, but
if you really want to know, it's made with
shark liver oil. Fish are attracted to it.
If you guys want some on your line, we can
probably catch our limit in a little while.

Or you can continue to drag your lines through the water so you don't have to clean fish."

It wasn't long until we had our limit and the guys were ready to call it a day. The men decided to keep the boat until the next day, stop by the drug store and get some fish ointment, and be on the lake early the next morning. We were having a big fish fry the next evening and needed plenty of fish. We were big fish eaters when they were fried in beer batter, or when Dick fixed Cajun style, blackened fish.

The fish fry was a huge success. We brought along our own camp stoves, special made for cooking fish. Norma was the cook and nobody tried to take her job away from her. The rest of us fixed salads and dessert and John made two big skillets of his fried potatoes. It was a cholesterol pig-out.

Beryl started passing out chocolate mints that tasted like a laxative I had tried once before. "I thought everybody would want to clean all the cholesterol out of their system as quickly as possible," she said.

Then we hopped into the cars and descended on the bar at the Pioneer Hotel where we danced to country music until midnight.

We discussed what time to rise the next morning for the Laughlin adventure. "We'll take the van and one other car, and leave at 8 o'clock," Waldo said. That way we won't be too crowded. Part of the group may want to come home before the others are ready. If I have a hot streak going, I don't leave for anything."

Chapter Seventeen

GAMBLER'S PARADISE

We were up early again, scurrying around, preparing for our big day in Laughlin, Nevada. We had never been there so it would be a new experience for us. But most of our group had been to Laughlin and were experts on how to beat the system...if there is such an expert. Laughlin's gambling revenues are closing in on Reno's as the third highest in the United States, after Atlantic City and Las Vegas.

We rode with John in his car and decided to take a side trip, an hour's journey into the past. Oatman Arizona's permanent residents number around 100, but because of a rich gold mine, the town once had a booming population of 10,000. Tourists enjoy visiting Oatman to relive its history. Saloons, shops and general stores have had their fronts restored and you can feel the good old days come back to life as you walk along the wooden sidewalks. A large array of items from hand-wovens to jewelry, American Indian crafts, antiques, goodies, and souvenirs are for sale in the little stores. Dramatizations of old-west shootouts are held twice a day. Wild burros, descendants from the early mining-day burros, roam the streets looking for a handout. You can purchase food for them in the stores for a small price.

"I just found out you can adopt a wild burro," I told our group. "Maybe we should look into it before we come back next year. We can haul him on the back porch of our motorhome. My grandkids could enjoy him in the spring and summer months, and we'll put him to work in the winter."

When I saw the burros coming into the edge of town, I went into the General Store and bought burro food. I walked up to one expecting him to eat the cubes of food out of my hand like a squirrel or a lamb. He was a very rude critter and grabbed the whole sack of food out of my hand, stomped it, with his foot tearing the sack, and proceeded to eat it all in two gulps. Then he looked at me as if to say, "Is that all you have?" I think if I hadn't moved out of the way he might have stomped me and had me for lunch. The store owners have to keep their doors closed or the burros walk right in.

"I don't think we want to adopt a burro. We'll have to find a more modern way of hauling gold dust up and down the mountain," my mate said.

Part of the journey to Oatman is on historic Route 66. As we traveled east of

Oatman, we drove quite slowly over the narrow, winding, bumpy, deteriorating road. At one point you could see the tracks of the Beale wagon trail and hand-hewn steps up a cliff to a natural spring. There's also a place where you can look for fire agates for a small fee, and visit a General Store to quench your thirst or hunger.

We were soon back onto the highway heading for our day in Laughlin and another promise of Paradise. All we had to do was win the big jackpot! With ten of us still in the group, surely one of us would walk away with a fortune.

Laughlin, which is an unincorporated town, has no mayor, city council, police force, or hospital. New schools were to open in 1991. What it does have are huge, brightly colored casinos looming along the slow-moving Colorado River. The casinos shake, roar and ring 24 hours a day, drawing people and their money from all over the west. Along Casino Drive there seems to be a never-ending construction boom. In 1980 the population of Laughlin was 94. In 1990 it was 4400.

Swarms of dirt-caked workers mingle with senior citizens, as the sound of money and coins clanking into the stainless steel trays on the slot machines, draws all kinds of people from all walks of life. The highways are jammed with RV's, limousines, and vehicles of all kinds blending into the traffic with cement mixers and bulldozers.

Most of the people clogging the roads to Laughlin in the wintertime aren't the usual gambler type. They are retired from a lifetime of hard work, and now have the money and the time to spend in the parking lots, living in their RV's and keeping the casinos busy. They bet modest amounts at the blackjack tables and spend hours at the slot machines.

     As we walked into the Colorado Belle, we
were greeted again with the sights and sounds
of senior citizens having the time of their
life. Whoops   of   joy   filled   our   ears,
accompanied by   the   clanging   coins   and
flashing lights that signal a pay off.
     The average Laughlin visitor, according
to a study last year by the Las Vegas
Convention Bureau,   is 56 years old and
budgets $353 for gambling. They are not the
ordinary Vegas-type high rollers. They are
senior citizens or Snowbirds.
     We   decided to   take   in one of the
advertised   specials of a 69 cent breakfast
before   we   started   our hard work of winning
money. We had to spend 20 minutes standing
in line, so some of us started playing the
slots   while   we   waited.   I had two dollars
worth of quarters I'd been saving for the
laundromat, and quickly shoved them into the
machine. "Look what I did! Look what I

did!" I shouted. I had hit a $100 jackpot on
the second pull as the lights started
flashing and the coins came pouring out.

"Don't leave your machine!" Beverly
hollered. "Most of the time when you hit a
jackpot the machines are geared to pay off
again right away. If you don't win after
playing five more dollars, then pick up your
winnings and find another machine."

That was my first tip. The second was
sure to follow. "Watch people as they play
the machines. If they've been playing quite
a while and walk away, you should grab their
machine and play it," Beryl said.

After breakfast we all went our separate
ways, but were to meet at the lounge in the
Riverside at four o'clock. "If you have a
game that's paying good, stay with it, we'll
find you," Waldo said.

Beverly and I tried our hand at blackjack
and I was doing pretty good for a novice. I
had won as many times as I lost, so was
hanging about even. We had the pit boss
excited several times as he kept coming over
to check out the game. I honestly think he
thought we were cheating.

"I don't know enough about the game to
cheat," I told Beverly.

"That's O.K. Just don't let them know
you don't know anything."

It wasn't long until I was losing, so I
headed for the roulette table. This is
another game where you can fool the dealer
into thinking you are an experienced player.
I picked my numbers randomly and started
stacking up a good pile of chips. I had no
idea what I was doing, all I knew was that I
was winning every time. Others at the table
started walking away until I was the only one
left. I was beginning to think I had B.O.
Then the dealer started trying to get me to
bet more money. He was doing it quietly so
the pit boss wouldn't see him. I had to

ponder the idea for awhile, but kept placing
my 50 cent bets.   Norma walked up and placed
a bet and wanted to know if I wanted to join
her at the crap table. "Sure, why not," I
said. "I don't know any more about craps
than I do about this." As I was leaving the
dealer just stood and shook his head. He
knew I was a novice. I had cashed in $40
more than I started with. It could have been
thousands of dollars if I had listened to
him.

Now that I was getting the hang of what
gambling was all about, we headed for the
crap table. The whole game was Greek to me,
but Norma was helping me place my bets. The
next time Norma's turn to throw the dice came
up, she was winning every time. We were
stacking up the chips again. About that time
a couple of smart alec old guys started
giving us a bad time.

"Hey mister," I said. "We may not know
much about the game, but we were smart enough
to bring our body guard with us, if you don't
leave us alone I'll call him. He's standing
right behind you." They both looked and
immediately changed their tone of voice and
attitude. Our body guard was Dick, I had
just spotted him before this happened. Dick
is one of those "big ole, good ole" boys that
belongs to our group. He stands 6' 8" tall
and weighs in at 300 lbs. Norma continued
rolling the dice and we made a total of $30
apiece. We should have been betting more.

When it was my turn to throw the dice, I
gave them a big Nebraska heave and one die
landed on the floor. The pit boss was on us
immediately.

"Don't ever do that again!" he commanded.
The stick man crawled under the furniture to
retrieve the dice and returned it to the pit
boss. He looked the dice over good, bit
them, threw them in the air, then ordered a
new set for the table.

"Did he think we were going to throw in some loaded dice?" I asked Norma. About that time Dick walked up to the table and suggested we might want to move on. Which we did. "How did you happen to be there when we needed you?" Norma asked him.

"I saw you girls walk over to that crap table. I thought I would watch to see how long it took you to get in trouble. It didn't take too long," Dick answered.

"Thanks for being there for us, you came in handy," I said.

We ran into Beryl and LaVern who had been playing the dime slots. "I've been playing this same machine all day and I'm still ahead a little bit so I'm going to play until it pays off," LaVern said.

Margaret came by looking for Eddie. She hadn't seen him all day and was worried about him. "Maybe he found a game that's paying good. If he did, he won't want to leave it. He's supposed to be one of my body guards and he's not doing his job," Margaret said.

We were having a good time wandering from one casino to another, shopping in the gift shops and stopping now and then to drop some more money in a one armed bandit.

Cork had been sitting at the same poker machine all day putting quarters in and staying about even. "Don't you find it kind of boring?" I asked.

"No, as long as I have a place to sit down and I'm not losing a bunch of money I'm satisfied," he said.

"Well, I'm going over and try the dollar machines. I've been winning all day, with my luck I'll probably hit a thousand dollar jackpot," I said.

"You'll lose it all," he said.

I found a machine that I was sure would make me rich in short order and started pumping silver dollars into it. I had only spent $20 of my winnings when the lady next

to me, leaning on a walker, lost her grip on
a machine and fell on the floor. I tried to
help her up, but she was too heavy. A
security guard arrived, helped her into a
wheel chair and wheeled her away. "Don't
forget my winnings," she hollered.

I worked with that machine until I had
spent $50 and had nothing to show for it, so
I quit and headed back to the Riverside where
we were supposed to meet at 4 o'clock. Norma
had just won a big pot on the dollar machine
and wasn't ready to go for dinner. She was
sure she would soon win more. Waldo was at a
blackjack table stacking up the chips. The
rest of the group was all standing around
like they had lost their last dime. "Why is
everyone so happy?" Beryl asked.

"It didn't take us long to spend our
money," Bill and John both said.

Margaret was still looking around for
Eddie, when he walked up to the crowd that
was gathering. "Where have you been?" she
wanted to know.

"Well, it's a long, sad story," he said.
"I've had the runs all day from that laxative
Beryl gave us last night. I had to wash out
my drawers and I've been standing in the
men's room all afternoon trying to get them
dry under the hand dryer. All of you must
have been busy, I haven't seen anybody."

"My carload's going home after we take in
the buffet down at Sam's Town," John said.

Thousands of Snowbirds camp in the
parking lots of the casinos. They are busy
building more campgrounds, but most of the
casinos don't care if you park in the parking
lot. They'll let anyone in that has money in
his pocket. They are also building large
parking garages for cars, leaving the parking
lots open for more RVers.

"I thought all the crazy Snowbirds were
in Quartzsite, Yuma and Lake Havasu," Cork
said. "But there's thousands and thousands

of them here, too."

There is hardly elbow room inside the casinos. We just happened to be there on Monday when it wasn't so busy. The hotels bring in big tour busses from California, Arizona and other bordering states. Why is it people almost go crazy getting into a place to lose their money? I heard one guy say, "You should have been here over the weekend, we had to fight to get a machine."

We sat down to a buffet fit for a king or for Snowbirds or anyone else. The cost, $5.98. We walked out, stuffed again.

"I don't know about you guys but I've had enough gambling," Cork said, "I don't mind coming for the day once in a while, but I sure wouldn't want to live out in the parking lot in a motorhome for weeks at a time just to have a place to spend my money."

"Some of the elderly people do that just so they can eat the cheap food and get the free drinks. Others might be compulsive gamblers or alcoholics and some just like all the excitement that goes with a place like this, "LaVern said.

We left Laughlin at 6 p.m. and pulled into the campground at 8 o'clock. We were worn out again, it had been another hard day of practicing our retirement.

Chapter Eighteen

TIME TO GO HOME

We had spent the last month searching one small part of Arizona for the ideal place for our retirement. Now it was time for us to start working our way back towards the cold country and back to the daily grind. We gathered our group together one more time to say good-bye.

Dick and Beverly, Eddie and Margaret were going through Las Vegas on their way home to see if they could win back some of the money they lost in Laughlin. John and LaVern were heading for Palm Springs, California, looking for plush golf courses and a place where the grass was green and the flowers bloomed all winter long. Bill and Beryl were ready to go back to Yuma and try to get their retirement back in order after having it disrupted for the last month.

Waldo and Norma, Cork and I had been invited to the Phoenix area to look over some of the mobile home parks there. Lloyd and Donna Haack from Dix, Nebraska, were staying in a new park in Mesa, Arizona. They wanted us to stop by and see what their idea of retirement was.

As we gathered one more time to share our views on the ideal place for retirement, it was plain to see that each couple had their own idea of what they wanted to do. I think we all knew when the final poll was taken, we would end up going our separate ways. But there's one thing we all agreed on and that was to meet every year in Quartzsite at Pow Wow time. Maybe some of us will end up boondocking in the winters around Quartzsite. Or maybe we will find a home in one of the many mobile home parks in the Quartzsite area. There are still many places we haven't investigated yet, many things we haven't had time to do. That, and the helpful, neighborly, year-round residents and the many friendly Snowbirds who flock to this area every winter, are what will keep us coming back year after year. As the old saying goes: "There are no strangers here, just friends we haven't met."

Quartzsite officially became a town on Tuesday, August 29, 1989. Richard Oldham was elected the first mayor, It can't be easy to have your population grow from 2,000 in the summer to 50,000 when the Snowbirds start migrating, and close to 1,000,000 the week of the Pow Wow. The town has growing pains, and trying to keep a town running smoothly hasn't been easy, as the town council has found out. There are problems, but the council is doing a good job of keeping the town moving forward. Just because it gets hot in the summer doesn't mean everyone hibernates like we do in Nebraska when it's cold. The town is constantly building and improving. There has to be someone working year round because every year when we return we find construction has been going on all summer. Quartzsite in September, 1991, opened a new school. One of the grocery stores was badly damaged in a fire. I expect there will be a new store when we return in 1992.

The Westrend's Security Group has plans to construct a 224-bed jail facility in Quartzsite. It will be the first privately owned and publicly operated facility in the

United States.   The   facility will generate
direct payroll benefits of $1,000,000 dollars
per   year   into the Quartzsite   economy.   It
will   provide   jobs   for 60 to 90 people.   So
Quartzsite is constantly on the move.

The people who   make   up   the   Quartzsite
Improvement   Association deserve   a   national
award   for   their   work in putting on the Pow
Wow   and   all   the   other   projects   they
undertake.   The   Quartzsite   Firefighters
Association,   the   ambulance   crews   and
emergency medical teams have to be a special,
well-trained group.   I don't   know   how   they
find their way through the mobs of people and
traffic to make   crisis   calls, but they do a
fantastic job.

Our   group,   while   sitting   around   the
campfire   one   evening   thought   of   several
things we would   like   to   see in the town of
Quartzsite.   In 1989 the council of the newly
formed   town   agreed   that   water,   sewer,
sidewalks, paved   streets and a park would be
their   #1 priority.   I know   the   council   is
working   on   all these important things.   The
park has been started and we agree that paved
streets,   sidewalks   and   sewer   are   badly
needed.   Maybe   they   don't want to know what
would draw even   more   people   to their area.
If   I were working any of the   businesses   in
Quartzsite   during   Pow   Wow time, I wouldn't
want to know what   would bring in more people
either.   But   here   are some suggestions   from
weary boondockers:

1.   A   portable,   traveling hot tub business.
This is needed so that people who walk up and
down the aisles of the shows,   all day, every
day,   can   soak   their   weary   bones.   Also,
necessary for Snowbirds who sit in the middle
of a cholla cactus.
2.   We suggest more resting areas   for   tired
ganders   at   all the shows.   The Pow Wow does
have   a nice resting   area.   Lady   Snowbirds

would be able to buy more if there were a
place for their mates to sit and wait.
3. Send a delegation to Branson, Missouri,
to invite some of the owners of Country
Western Music Theaters to build theaters in
Quartzsite for their winter home. Some of
the entertainers are getting older and don't
like the idea of taking their show on the
road in the wintertime. They might as well
join the rest of us Snowbirds.
4. Invite some well known gospel singers and
evangelists to put on a nightly crusade.
Snowbirds would pack the place every night.
In the ball game of life, most Snowbirds are
living in the last quarter. They don't have
a lot of time left to sort out priorities.
Some of us still haven't found the peace
we've been looking for. We haven't found
Paradise. Branson is full of good, gospel
singing groups. Somewhere around here there
should be someone with a gold mine, ready to
invest enough money to build a large stadium
or arena.
4. The traffic continues to be a problem,
but the four-way stops are working as good as
any stop light. Maybe a turning lane would
help the congestion.
5. Have your fund raising event for the
homeless people of your area during Snowbird
Mating Season, so we can do our part to help.

Then there's a want list of things we
could use to spice up our own group:

1. Wanted, someone who is really musically
inclined. They must be able to play a guitar
and sing, too.
2. Wanted, a retired preacher who would like
to join a bunch of sinners and hold church
service on Sunday, and a hymn sing-a-long on
Wednesday nights.
3. We have two single lady Snowbirds looking
for mates. Beverly's bringing her mother

next year.   Maude   is   85 years old,   been
married four times and has outlived them all.
She figures she's got enough life left in her
for one more husband.   Cork's sister is
coming next year. Rose is looking for one of
the younger, retired men that likes to enjoy
life to the fullest. She's a good cook and
enjoys eating,   traveling, and fishing...she
has her own boat. (No, she's not fat.)
4. Wanted, a good cook who can have supper
ready when we arrive home in the evening
after walking around the shows all day. We
may have to keep Rose for this job. It is
possible that one man could fill all of the
above needs if he is a musically inclined,
retired preacher who likes to travel, fish,
cook, enjoy life and has his own RV.
5. One thing we've decided for sure, we must
have the makings for a cream can dinner...
something to take the place of beans once in
a while. To make a cream can dinner you need
an old fashioned cream can: Put smooth rocks
in the bottom with a screen over the rocks.
Wash the rocks first, or you can put
cornhusks in the bottom. This keeps the food
from sticking. Layer fresh corn on the cob,
new potatoes, carrots, cabbage, and onions,
then place Polish sausage on the top. Place
one big, new potato on top. When the potato
is done all the rest will be cooked. Dig a
hole (checking all the time for gold) and
build a fire so you will have a good bed of
coals, then set the can onto the coals and
wait three hours. The cream can works like a
pressure cooker. The juice from the meat
cooks all through the can, flavoring the
vegetables. Ironwood will make an excellent
bed of coals for the cream can. One can will
serve 20 people. We have the cream can.
Anyone who has the fresh garden vegetables is
invited for supper.
     "Maybe we ought to open our own little
eating place and sell cream can dinners,"

Waldo said.
    "We'll have to think on that one for a while," John answered.
    After we received our hugs all around, we parted company and headed in different directions. Waldo and Norma, Cork and I turned east on Interstate 10, our destination, Mesa, Arizona. We arrived in Mesa at the Valle del Oro Mobile Home Park in time to be invited to a potluck dinner. Valle del Oro is a complete, private community recreation complex. All their guests are provided with a social and activity calendar that is second to none. We were told that the friendly staff and our new neighbors would welcome us to a great new world of recreation. "We are big enough so you'll never feel crowded...just part of a fun-loving crowd," says their brochure.

It was like walking into an oasis after wandering in the desert for weeks. There was a light breeze and the palm trees were swaying as the lights were reflecting off the calming, blue waters of the pools. "OOHH! this is what I want," Norma said. "You can have the desert, I'm not going any further than right here."

The list of activities was similar, but longer than any other place we had been. There were two swimming pools, plus a lap pool, tennis courts, billiards, standing gym, horseshoe courts, shuffle board courts, and a large ballroom with all kinds of dance lessons. There was a putting green, organized golf at area courses, aerobics, ceramics, painting, lapidary, silversmithing, sewing, carpentry, bingo, special theme parties, big band dances, holiday events, talent nights, seminars, potlucks, barbecues, snack bar and a country store every week.

"I don't know if I can keep up here," Cork said. "You certainly won't get bored. If you do, it's your own fault."

In this park you can buy a park model trailer or stay in your own RV. Something more for us to think about. We haven't decided yet if we're ready to buy a park model. We want to be free to travel and maybe at a later date we'll be tired of traveling and be ready to settle in one place for the winter.

We stayed a week relaxing in luxury. We rinsed the last of the desert from our bodies by swimming and soaking in the hot tub every day. As we watched the people coming and going, joining in from time to time in their activities, it made us realize that these people are jamming as many activities into each day as they possibly can, or as many as they want to. Some of them are doing things they never had time to do when they were working and raising a family. They are learning new hobbies and taking part in new recreation. In short, staying healthy, and keeping the old heart pumping right along.

I was looking back over our life and could see that as we grow older we become busier. The months seem to push each other rudely out of the way as the years slip off the calendar. It seems only yesterday that we were married and right away had three children to worry about raising. Now our grandsons are growing up and we are realizing they don't have a lot of time for grandma and grandpa either. So, what do we do? Find our own excitement, join in the fun, and enjoy life to the fullest while we still can.

"I haven't been looking forward to retirement because I didn't think I could handle having Waldo around 24 hours a day," Norma said. "What were we going to do besides sit and look at each other? Since I've seen how they live in this mobile home park, and all the activities they provide, I think I can handle it. There are things we can do together and some things we can do separately. I can hardly wait to come back next year."

Beryl had been trying to warn us about retirement. "For us, retirement was just like getting married all over again," she said. "I had Bill around all the time, and I wasn't used to that. He was a trucker and was gone long stretches at a time. We had a lot of adjusting to do."

"Some of the people we talked to had sold everything they owned and tried RVing full-time," Bill said. "We talked about it, but the first thing Beryl wanted to know was what part of my stuff I was willing to give up. I couldn't give up all my toys. My motorcycle, my boat, my guns, my coin collection are all important to me and I can't part with them. That put an end to our talk about full timing." So Beryl and Bill chose to buy a house in Yuma for their retirement, just one more option open to the Snowbird.

Each year Snowbirds join the mass exodus from north to south as they return to the same area and join their flock of friends. There has to be a big turnover of people in the mobile home parks as Snowbirds grow older and die. The ones who die are exiting this world happy because they've been coming here to the warm country, where Snowbird Mating Season keeps them mobile, eager and enjoying life right up to the end.

THE END

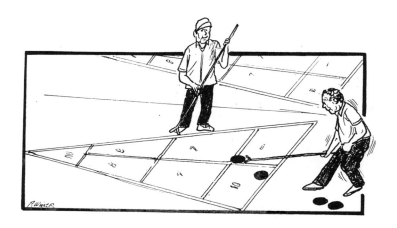

EPILOGUE

Two of our grandsons are in the second grade. Preston and John were asked to write a story about their grandparents. Together, this is what they wrote.

When the snow starts to fall and the streets get icy gramma and grampa pack all the food and water and clothes they have into the camper and fly south with a bunch of their old friends. Gramma says it's because grampa is practicing his retardment. All their friends are retarded too. When they are gone they send us postcards and tell us about what they are doing. They go to a place called Quartseye and hang around with their retarded friends in the desert.

They go to flea markets and grampa says gramma buys all the fleas she can find. Grampa says they are saving so much money that he has to make a trip to the bank every day to deposit it all.

Grampa says gramma is doing exercises trying to keep from getting fat. But, it's not working. She eats too much stuff at the flea market. Gramma and her friends are doing a lot of walking trying to keep in shape. We tried to get gramma to buy some high tops, but she wouldn't do it. Grampa doesn't think gramma knows how to cook any more. We don't think so either. She doesn't make cookies, she goes to Mexico and buys them. She's too busy to bake.

Sometimes grampa thinks little boys should be seen and not heard. Sometimes gramma thinks grampa should be seen and not heard.

Gramma has a sweatshirt that makes her a member of "The Grammas On The Go Club". She's always busy doing something and she has a different sweat shirt for everything she does. She has one for golf, for bowling, for playing bridge, one to wear in Quartseye and even one with hearts and clubs on it to wear to Las Vegas.

Grampa got mad when someone in the Quartseye paper called his camper an outhouse on wheels. We've never seen an outhouse, but gramma says they have a honey bucket that pumps out their toilet and sells ice cream cones.

We're always glad to see gramma and grampa come home because they have their camper stacked full of stuff for us. Last year when they came home grampa drove in the yard and he had a donkey on the back porch and gramma was sitting in a rocking chair on top of the motorhome. Grampa mumbled something about gramma buying too much stuff and there wasn't room in the camper for it, so he tied her and the rocking chair on top. We think someone pulled the people plug in Quartseye so them and their retarded friends had to come home. Gramma says she had so much fun she's going to write a book about it.

A GREAT STOPPING OFF PLACE

I'd like to issue a special invitation to all RVer's who travel Interstate 80. When you are traveling through Western Nebraska, take time to stop in Kimball, the Western gateway to Nebraska, for a free night's camping at the Gotte Park located on the eastern edge of town on Highway 30. You will recognize the park when you see a giant, obsolete Titan I missle on display. It stands 100 feet tall. Kimball is 64 miles east of Cheyenne, Wyoming, and 150 miles northeast of Denver, Colorado.

You'll enjoy the pleasant weather in Kimball in the summer and fall. Western Nebraska evenings are cool and quiet. If you're looking for the ideal place to spend your summers where the air is clean and there is no big city traffic we invite you to try Kimball. There are plenty of Mobile Home Parks. We are just a bunch of down home country folks ready to make you feel right at home. Kimball has one of the best, well-groomed golf courses you'll find anywhere.

Kimball's big celebration is called Farmer's Day and is held the second Saturday in September every year. There's free barbecue sandwiches and trimmings for all. When you start your migration south next year and need a resting and feeding place You're welcome to try Kimball, the Oil Capitol of Nebraska and Missle Center USA.

Travel Notes

Travel Notes

Travel Notes